D1378876

The Unabomber

by Diane Yancey

LUCENT BOOKS

An imprint of Thomson Gale, a part of The Thomson Corporation

THOMSON
™
GALE

Detroit • New York • San Francisco • New Haven, Conn. • Waterville, Maine • London

© 2007 Thomson Gale, a part of The Thomson Corporation.

Thomson and Star Logo are trademarks and Gale and Lucent Books are registered trademarks used herein under license.

For more information, contact
Lucent Books
27500 Drake Rd.
Farmington Hills, MI 48331-3535
Or you can visit our Internet site at http://www.gale.com

LIBRARY OF CONGRESS CATALOGING-IN-PUBLICATION DATA

Yancey, Diane.
  The Unabomber / by Diane Yancey.
    p. cm. — (Crime scene investigations)
  Includes bibliographical references and index.
  ISBN-13: 978-1-59018-992-4 (hardcover)
  1. Kaczynski, Theodore John, 1942– 2. Bombing investigation—United States—Case studies. 3. Bombings—United States—Case studies. 4. Bombers (Terrorists)—United States—Case studies. I. Title.
  HV8079.B62Y36 2007
  364.152'3092—dc22
  [B]
                                                                2007015979

ISBN-10: 1-59018-992-2
Printed in the United States of America

Contents

Foreword

The popularity of crime scene and investigative crime shows on television has come as a surprise to many who work in the field. The main surprise is the concept that crime scene analysts are the true crime solvers, when in truth, it takes dozens of people, doing many different jobs, to solve a crime. Often, the crime scene analyst's contribution is a small one. One Minnesota forensic scientist says that the public "has gotten the wrong idea. Because I work in a lab similar to the ones on *CSI*, people seem to think I'm solving crimes left and right—just me and my microscope. They don't believe me when I tell them that it's the investigators that are solving crimes, not me."

Crime scene analysts do have an important role to play, however. Science has rapidly added a whole new dimension to gathering and assessing evidence. Modern crime labs can match a hair of a murder suspect to one found on a murder victim, for example, or recover a latent fingerprint from a threatening letter, or use a powerful microscope to match tool marks made during the wiring of an explosive device to a tool in a suspect's possession.

Probably the most exciting of the forensic scientist's tools is DNA analysis. DNA can be found in just one drop of blood, a dribble of saliva on a toothbrush, or even the residue from a fingerprint. Some DNA analysis techniques enable scientists to tell with certainty, for example, whether a drop of blood on a suspect's shirt is that of a murder victim.

While these exciting techniques are now an essential part of many investigations, they cannot solve crimes alone. "DNA doesn't come with a name and address on it," says the Minnesota forensic scientist. "It's great if you have someone in custody to match the sample to, but otherwise, it doesn't help. That's the investigator's job. We can have all the great DNA evidence in the world, and without a suspect, it will just sit on the shelf. We've all seen cases with very little forensic evidence get solved by the resourcefulness of a detective."

While forensic specialists get the most media attention today, the work of detectives still forms the core of most criminal investigations. Their job, in many ways, has changed little over the years. Most cases are still solved through the persistence and determination of a criminal detective whose work may be anything but glamorous. Many cases require routine, even mind-numbing tasks. After the July 2005 bombings in London, for example, police officers sat in front of video players watching thousands of hours of closed-circuit television tape from security cameras throughout the city, and as a result were able to get the first images of the bombers.

The Lucent Books Crime Scene Investigations series explores the variety of ways crimes are solved. Titles cover particular crimes such as murder, specific cases such as the killing of three civil rights workers in Mississippi, or the role specialists such as medical examiners play in solving crimes. Each title in the series demonstrates the ways a crime may be solved, from the various applications of forensic science and technology to the reasoning of investigators. Sidebars examine both the limits and possibilities of the new technologies and present crime statistics, career information, and step-by-step explanations of scientific and legal processes.

The Crime Scene Investigations series strives to be both informative and realistic about how members of law enforcement—criminal investigators, forensic scientists, and others—solve crimes, for it is essential that student researchers understand that crime solving is rarely quick or easy. Many factors—from a detective's dogged pursuit of one tenuous lead to a suspect's careless mistakes to sheer luck to complex calculations computed in the lab—are all part of crime solving today.

Eighteen-Year Manhunt

Just after noon on May 15, 1985, graduate student John E. Hauser walked across the University of California at Berkeley campus, entered the engineering building, and made his way to the computer lab. Hauser, a captain in the U.S. Air Force, was studying electrical engineering while waiting to hear if he had been accepted into the National Aeronautics and Space Administration's (NASA) astronaut training program in Houston, Texas.

When he entered the lab Hauser saw a three-ring binder sitting on one of the unoccupied tables. The binder was perched on top of a small plastic box, attached by a rubber band. Hauser assumed that another student had accidentally left it behind. He opened the binder to look for a name, but its pages were blank, so he lifted the lid of the box. When he did, it exploded. Hauser was hit by shards of metal, nail fragments, lead, and double-pointed tacks that were part of the bomb. The force of the blast tore the fingers off his right hand. His Air Force Academy ring was hurled across the room so hard that the word "Academy" was imprinted on the opposite wall. Hauser later said, "I was standing at the table and there was a chair between me and the bomb. I think that caught a lot of the blast. It could easily have killed me, given the force of the explosion."[1]

Hearing the explosion, other people in the building rushed to Hauser's aid and called an ambulance. The engineering student was taken to the hospital, where doctors worked to save his life. They were ultimately successful, but Hauser lost most of the sight in one eye and the use of his right hand. He was forced to give up his flying career as well as his dreams of going into space. He later observed, "I could become very bitter, I suppose. But life's too precious for that. . . . There's too many wonderful things for me to spend too much time, too much energy thinking about the Unabomber."[2]

Hunt for a Killer

The Unabomber: The name was deeply frustrating to investigators who had hunted the cunning and elusive killer since 1978. And there was no question that Hauser was one of his victims. The letters "FC," stamped on a piece of metal found in the wreckage of the computer lab, were the bomber's trademark, imprinted on virtually all of his devices since 1980.

Greater security measures were enacted at Los Angeles International Airport in 1995 after the Unabomber threatened to blow up an airplane.

ALL
BAGS
ARE
SUBJECT

The Unabomber's campaign of terror stretched over seventeen years.

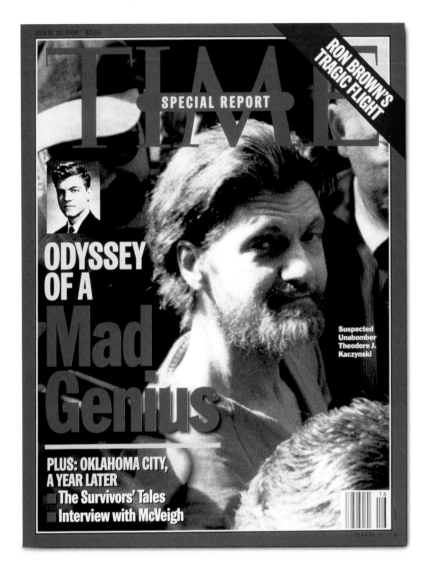

Hauser was the eighteenth person to be injured by the Unabomber, named for the universities and airlines he targeted. Like so many other Unabomber victims, the engineering student had been a casualty of a device left in a public place, threatening any innocent passerby who picked it up. Like the others, he had only been injured, although more severely than anyone before. Apparently the bomber was becoming more skilled as time passed. His cruelty, unpredictability, and mobility left many

Americans fearing they could be his next victim. "I wish we could just catch this guy and put an end to this," said a worried mother in Los Angeles after the bomber threatened to blow up an airliner in 1995. "How do you feel secure anymore with this terrorism? . . . It's a different world from the one I grew up in."[3]

The best law enforcement agencies in the nation spent $50 million and thousands of man-hours in an attempt to catch the bomber. They analyzed crime scenes. They went to scrap metal businesses where he might have bought parts. They visited libraries with subpoenas to see who checked out books having to

The Chameleon

For years Americans knew the Unabomber as a sketch on a wanted poster, almost unrecognizable behind his hooded sweatshirt and aviator sunglasses. Even investigators who hunted him were baffled by his furtiveness, as Robert Graysmith explains in his book Unabomber: A Desire to Kill:

He was a shadow barely seen and never heard—or many shadows. The FBI file actually contemplated that the prey might be not one man but many complex individuals. He was a chameleon [changeable] eluding the police because he kept his own counsel and each day became something new. It was hard to fault the authorities—there had never been anything like him before. . . .

In the end the FBI was no closer to catching him than in the beginning. Only their final and desperate strategy, to encourage the bomber to explain himself and to finally involve the public in the chase, would prove the Unabomber's undoing.

Robert Graysmith, *Unabomber: A Desire to Kill.* Washington, DC: Regnery, 1997, p. xiv.

do with bombs and bomb making. They consulted psychics. A $1 million reward was offered, tip lines were set up for the public to call with their suspicions, and hundreds of suspects were interviewed. In the end, mountains of information were amassed, but no suspect was identified. Max Noel of the Federal Bureau of Investigation (FBI) recalled, "This case itself was an info-management nightmare because we had *too much* information."[4]

An Important Message

The Unabomber's manifesto, sent to newspapers in 1995, gave America a better understanding of the killer's motives. Nancy Gibbs, Richard Lacayo, Lance Morrow, Jill Smolowe, and David Van Biema present the essence of his message in Mad Genius: The Odyssey, Pursuit, and Capture of the Unabomber Suspect:

"If we had never done anything violent . . . and had submitted the present writings to a publisher, they probably would not have been accepted. If they had been accepted and published, they probably would not have attracted many readers, because it's more fun to watch the entertainment put out by the media than to read a sober essay." And the message, he believed was too important to be ignored: industrial society was a plague; it was destroying souls, disrupting community, ravaging nature, ruining the promise of a country in love with its fantasy of the frontier. "In order to get our message before the public with some chance of making a lasting impression," wrote a man who never was able to make a lasting impression, "we've had to kill people."

Nancy Gibbs, Richard Lacayo, Lance Morrow, Jill Smolowe, and David Van Biema, *Mad Genius: The Odyssey, Pursuit, and Capture of the Unabomber Suspect.* New York: Warner, 1996, p. 13.

A Difficult Road

At times years went by without hearing from the bomber. Investigators hoped that he was in prison or had perhaps blown himself up with one of his own devices. He always resurfaced, however, striking with renewed force before disappearing back into the shadows. "There's been no other criminal like this that I know of," James A. Fox, former dean of the College of Criminal Justice at Northeastern University in Boston, observed. "There are many criminal cases that remain unsolved. But here is one that went on for 18 years, in which the killer remained at large and continued his trade without apprehension. That takes an enormous amount of cunning."[5]

Then, when it seemed likely that the case would never be solved, the bomber began communicating with his enemies. His demands eventually led to a controversial law enforcement experiment, a difficult decision, and a long-anticipated arrest. "Everyone involved in this case is . . . eternally indebted to the heroic actions of David Kaczynski,"[6] prosecutor Robert J. Cleary stated after the bomber had been arrested.

Who David Kaczynski was, his relationship to the bomber, and the difficult road he traveled to help bring the killer to justice mesmerized the nation from 1996 until 1998. Those years were filled with pain and frustration for everyone associated with the case. The years were also filled, however, with intriguing revelations that made the story of the Unabomber one of the most unusual and compelling chapters of America's history.

CHAPTER 1

Targets Coast-to-Coast

From the first bombing on May 26, 1978, until the last deadly blast on April 24, 1995, investigators puzzled over how the Unabomber chose his targets, and who his next victim might be. Just when they thought they understood his objectives, he seemed to change focus. Then the investigators had to rethink their conclusions and try to decide again what the Unabomber wanted to achieve. Patrick Fischer, who escaped injury in a 1982 bombing, observed, "He always has some new wrinkle, just enough so that his MO [method of operating] is basically the same. But with just enough variety among the choice of victims that it's very hard to get a common denominator and solve the case."[7]

Wrong Place, Wrong Time

The Unabomber's first victim was Terry Marker, a security officer at Northwestern University in Evanston, Illinois. It was obvious to everyone, however, that Marker had been injured only because he was in the wrong place at the wrong time.

On May 26, 1978, a package wrapped in brown paper was found in a parking lot on the University of Illinois's Chicago campus. The package was addressed to engineering professor Edward J. Smith at Rensselaer Polytechnic Institute in Troy, New York. The name Buckley Crist, a professor of engineering and materials science at Northwestern, was on the return address.

A thoughtful stranger picked up the package and called Crist, assuming he had lost it before he could mail it. Crist was puzzled because he did not know Smith and had not prepared a package for him. Nevertheless he arranged for it to be delivered to his office. Prudently, he also asked Marker to examine it before it was opened.

Marker was amused that anyone would think that such an ordinary-looking parcel might be dangerous. His amusement changed to horror, however, when he removed the brown paper and the box exploded in his hands. The device was not powerful enough to kill, but he had to be taken to a nearby hospital where his hands were treated for burns.

During the investigation that followed, the bomb squad found such mundane items as match heads, rubber bands, and nails among the remains of the bomb. Both Smith and Crist were interviewed, but both denied any knowledge of the package or who might have sent it. Investigators were left with no leads, treated the incident as a prank, and shortly thereafter discarded the remnants of the bomb.

A plain brown package similar to this one is how the Unabomber disguised his first bomb, which was set off on May 26, 1978.

The Second Victim

The 1978 bombing was still unsolved when, on May 9, 1979, another bomb exploded at Northwestern University. The victim—graduate student John G. Harris—was someone who was also in the wrong place at the wrong time. He had decided to check out the contents of a box that had been sitting for several days on a table on the second floor of Northwestern's Technological Institute.

The box looked odd. It was the size of a cigar box and covered with finger-sized pieces of unfinished wood that had been glued to its surface. When Harris opened the lid, it exploded, blowing off his glasses and sending smoke and dozens of match heads around the room.

While Harris was being treated for minor cuts and burns, investigators noted that the bomb had been constructed of such common items as flashlight batteries, matches, wooden dowels, and white glue. Despite similarities between the 1978 and 1979 bombings, however, no one made a connection between the incidents, and no arrest was made in the case.

In the Air

Six months after the second incident, a vastly different kind of attack led investigators to understand that a serial bomber was at work in Illinois. On November 15, 1979, American Airlines Flight 444, traveling between Chicago and Washington National Airport, was forced to make an emergency landing because of a fire in the cargo hold. The plane landed safely, but twelve passengers were taken to the hospital and treated for smoke inhalation.

Fire fighters who arrived on the scene located the source of the smoke—a pipe bomb in a bag of mail. The device had contained a modified barometer whose needle moved with changing pressure as the plane ascended. When the plane reached a certain altitude, the needle completed an electrical circuit and ignited a quantity of gunpowder. The bomb wall, however, had been a thin-walled juice can that had burst apart before pressure could build. The result had been a small fire rather than a hole blown through the side of the plane. Investigators felt certain that only luck—and the bomber's in-experience—had saved the lives of the passengers onboard.

Airline bombing is a federal crime, so the FBI was called into the case. The flight had originated in Chicago; thus, FBI agent and bomb specialist James "Chris" Ronay sent detailed

The Other Victims

The Unabomber's attacks had enormous repercussions for victims as well as their families. Consequences were particularly severe for Professor Diogenes Angelakos, as Robert Graysmith details in Unabomber: A Desire to Kill:

For Angelakos, the aftermath of the bombing brought more pain than the attack itself. Surgeons at Herrick Hospital [in Berkeley] attempted to repair Angelakos's ruptured tendons, but his right hand remained crippled. Far worse, the formerly sunny man was plagued by dark thoughts. Fear of another attempt on his life played upon him. . . .

He feared the turn of a key in the car ignition, an unbidden letter, or a birthday present left on his desk. He dreaded crank phone calls. Yet his own terror was nothing compared to the greatest tragedy in his life.

With his crippled right hand, Angelakos could no longer care for his ailing wife. Even worse . . . was that in his darkness he could no longer cheer her. Within a month she was dead.

Robert Graysmith, *Unabomber: A Desire to Kill.* Washington, DC: Regnery, 1997, pp. 100–101.

drawings of the bomb and its charred wrapping to the FBI field office and the U.S. postal inspection lab in that city. In an attempt to identify the maker of the device, those investigators contacted local police jurisdictions and found someone who remembered a similar crude pipe bomb found on the Northwestern campus in 1979.

Random Parts, Random Targets

Parts from the 1979 bomb had been saved, and a close comparison confirmed the similarities to the airliner bomb. Both were pipe bombs in boxes. Both had been made from household items like batteries and white glue. Both contained wood. Ronay said of the Northwestern bomb: "As soon as we looked at it, we made an identification. This was clearly made by the same guy that made the bomb on the airplane."[8]

Once the 1979 bombing was linked to the bomb on Flight 444, investigators decided to check the 1978 bombing on the Northwestern campus. This was more difficult, because the debris had been thrown away. Photos had been taken, however, and they revealed that this bomb, too, had been fashioned by the same person.

Now that the bombs were connected by their components, investigators tried to connect the victims in some way. Even though they appeared to have been targeted at random, their backgrounds were thoroughly checked in search of a common thread. There appeared to be none. They did not have the same friends, share the same interests, or attend the same classes, churches, or clubs. Apparently the bomber did not need to strike at a specific person in order to be satisfied.

By the Numbers

3,100

The number of tips phoned in on the FBI's toll-free Unabomber hotline in one week in December 1985.

"Dear Mr. Wood"

On June 10, 1980, however, the bomber put an end to the theory that his targets were always random. In an upscale neighborhood in Lake Forest, Illinois, United Airlines president Percy A. Wood found a package in the mailbox outside his home. The package was addressed to him, and he recognized the name on the return address: Enoch Fischer. Fischer had sent Wood a letter a few days earlier, telling him that he would soon receive a book that was of great social significance. The letter read in part: "Dear Mr. Wood, I am sending copies of 'Ice Brothers' by Sloan Wilson to a number of prominent people in the Chicago area, because I believe (this book) . . . should be read by all who make important decisions affecting the public welfare."[9]

Wood had no idea who Fischer was, but he took the package into the kitchen and peeled back the paper wrapping. Inside was indeed a copy of Wilson's novel, the story of two brothers

Police guard the home of Percy A. Wood, president and CEO of United Airlines, on June 10, 1980, after Wood was injured by a bomb sent by the Unabomber.

who face a variety of enemies off the coast of Greenland in World War II. Curious, Wood opened the volume. When he did, it exploded. Fragments of wood and metal shot outward, cutting and burning his face, hands, and legs. A section of galvanized pipe, part of the bomb wall, punched a large hole in the ceiling. Dazed and horrified, Wood staggered to a near-by neighbor for help. Laurie McCurdy, who called an ambulance, stated, "He told me he opened the package and 'it just blew.'" [10]

There was no doubt that Wood was the intended victim of the blast. While he recovered in the hospital, investigators tried to determine why he had been attacked. He had ties to the airline industry, which the bomber had previously targeted. But there were thousands of people who worked for the airlines. Why had Wood been specifically chosen? Postulating that the bomber had either read about him or met him sometime in the past, investigators added the incident to their file and continued with their investigation.

Danger on Campus

As the bomber struck repeatedly in the coming years, investigators drew several conclusions from his choice of targets. Because he did not always attack specific individuals, they believed that he held a grudge against someone or something that the victims represented. That definitely included institutions of higher learning. The bomber struck repeatedly on Northwestern University and the University of California campuses. He targeted Vanderbilt University, the University of Utah, and Yale University as well.

Within the university system, he struck those who worked with computers and technology. In October 1981, for instance, he planted a bomb outside a computer classroom on the University of Utah campus. Campus security officials were able to defuse the device and no one was injured. In May 1982 Patrick Fischer, head of the computer science department at Vanderbilt, was the recipient of a package bomb in the mail.

Fischer's secretary, Janet Smith, opened the package for him and had to be rushed to the hospital with severe injuries.

Five months later on July 2, 1982, engineering professor Diogenes J. Angelakos was seriously injured by an exploding device that he found in a common room of the engineering building at the University of California at Berkeley. Three years later Hauser met a similar fate in the same building. Also in 1985 research assistant Nicklaus Suino suffered burns and shrapnel wounds when he opened a package bomb disguised as a manuscript. It had been sent to University of Michigan professor James V. McConnell in Ann Arbor, Michigan. McConnell, a psychologist who specialized in human behavior modification, was also injured in the blast. "Who could hate me this much to send me a bomb?"[11] he asked himself, but could not come up with an answer.

In June 1993 a letter bomb exploded inside a Yale University building, pictured, injuring Professor David Gelernter.

Professor David Gelernter was injured by a letter bomb in June 1993.

In June 1993 Charles Epstein, a geneticist at the University of California, and computer scientist David Gelernter of Yale University in New Haven, Connecticut, were injured by bombs they received in the mail. Although in every case investigators did their best to determine why the bomber had chosen each specific individual, no one could come up with a conclusive motive. Fischer could only postulate: "For a while I thought he [the bomber] opened up *Who's Who* [reference books containing biographical data on notable individuals] and threw a dart until he got a computer scientist. That's probably wrong. There has to be a link."[12]

High-Tech Targets

The Unabomber attacked people at universities, but he also went after other targets. On June 13, 1985, a package bomb—not addressed to a specific person—was discovered in the mailroom of a Boeing Company facility in Auburn, Washington. Boeing is an aerospace and defense corporation based in Chicago, Illinois, and was involved in building airliners as well as high-tech projects like the space shuttle and the international space station. A bomb squad disabled the bomb before it could harm anyone and determined that it had been mailed from Oakland, California, just miles from Berkeley, where Hauser had been injured one month before.

Six months later, on December 11, 1985, the bomber struck again, and this time his bomb was powerful enough to kill. Sacramento resident and computer store owner Hugh C. Scrutton was on his way to lunch when he spotted what appeared to be a

Hugh Scrutton was the first victim to be killed by a Unabomber bomb, in December 1985.

block of wood with nails protruding from it in the parking lot behind his business. Afraid that someone would drive over it, he picked it up. It exploded in his face. Employees from nearby businesses raced to the scene but were too late to save Scrutton, who died before he could be taken to a hospital. "We found body parts of Hugh Scrutton on the roof,"[13] reported Sacramento police detective Robert Bell.

Bell and other investigators suspected that Scrutton had been targeted because of his ties to computers and technology but noted that, if such had been the case, the bomber had been extremely careless. The device had been left where people from neighboring businesses walked to and from their cars. Anyone could have picked the bomb up at any time with disastrous results.

If investigators doubted that a computer motive was behind the Sacramento bombing, that doubt was put to rest when the Unabomber struck in Salt Lake City, Utah, on February 20, 1987. Gary Wright, one of the owners of a computer store called CAAMS Inc., was injured in the parking lot at the rear entrance to his business when he kicked what he thought was a bag of boards with nails sticking out of them. Wright was not killed, but the bomb was powerful enough to inflict permanent damage. He described his feelings at the time: "At first I thought I'd been shot. It was just

By the Numbers

65

The number of arrests made by U.S. postal inspectors in response to mail bombs, threats, and hoaxes in 2005.

The Sketch

Investigators were elated when an eyewitness helped create a sketch of the Unabomber, but like many composite drawings, it had its short-comings. Profiler John Douglas explains in his book Unabomber: On the Trail of America's Most-Wanted Serial Killer, *coauthored with Mark Olshaker:*

The FBI sketch of the Unabomber, based on the recollection of Tammy Fluehe, a witness to the 1987 Salt Lake City, Utah, bombing.

I've never placed too much emphasis on the composite drawing. While they can be better than nothing, they are fairly generic. In the Unabomber composite not much of the actual face was showing. There would be too much of a tendency to rule out individuals who didn't have curly hair and wear sunglasses and hoods. I've interviewed guys in prison who told me they breathed a sigh of relief as soon as they saw the published composite because they realized it looked like any man on the street. It didn't resemble them enough to trigger an identification.

John Douglas and Mark Olshaker, *Unabomber: On the Trail of America's Most-Wanted Serial Killer.* New York: Pocket Books, 1996, p. 51.

this huge impact that hit me. The force of the impact knocked me back a good twelve to fifteen feet, and I started to go into shock. . . . There were quite a few holes in my body, and a lot of the 'bullets' in the top of the device came up and struck me under the neck."[14]

Eyewitness

The bombing in Salt Lake City not only confirmed that the Unabomber had a grudge against computer owners, it produced something that was unique up to that point—an eyewitness. The morning of the bombing Tammy Fluehe, a secretary working for CAAMS, happened to glance out a window overlooking the parking lot and noticed a man bending down between two parked cars.

As she watched, the man straightened and turned directly toward her. He was wearing aviator-style sunglasses that partially hid his face and a gray-hooded sweatshirt that covered his hair. Nevertheless, she could see that he was Caucasian, had a prominent jaw, thin mustache, and a ruddy complexion. She later estimated that the man was about thirty years old, nearly six feet (1.83m) tall and weighed about 165 pounds (75kg).

With Fluehe's help forensic artists created sketches of the perpetrator, which were printed and displayed. The effort proved fruitless, however. Investigators remained hopeful but had to admit that the bomber had so successfully disguised himself that even an eyewitness sighting was useless.

Ad executive Thomas Mosser became a victim of the Unabomber in December 1994.

Another Death

The year 1994 marked a new category of victims targeted by the Unabomber. On December 10 of that year, Thomas Mosser, a New York City advertising executive, was preparing to go shopping with his family for a Christmas tree, when he opened a package that had been mailed to his home. It was a bomb, packed with nails, razor blades, and other pieces of metal.

The explosion was tremendous, as Mosser's wife remembered:

> A thunderous noise resounded throughout the house . . . a white mist was pouring from the kitchen doorway . . . when the mist settled to

the floor, a horrifying image emerged. My husband's body, face up on the floor, his stomach slashed open, his face was partially blackened and distorted. Blood. Horror. . . . I dialed 911 and screamed 'I need an ambulance!'"[15]

For four months investigators puzzled over why the Unabomber had targeted the ad executive. On April 24, 1995, however, another killing claimed their attention. A package about the size of a shoebox was left outside the Sacramento office of the California Forestry Association (CFA), a group that had lobbied Congress to ease the Endangered Species Act, legislation which protected endangered animals and hampered logging in the Pacific Northwest. The package was addressed to William Dennison, former president of CFA, and appeared from its return address to have come from an Oakland furniture company.

Gilbert Murray, president of the California Forestry Association, was killed by a package bomb in April 1995.

"Running in Circles"

A CFA secretary took the package inside with the intention of forwarding it to Dennison. Gilbert Murray, CFA's current president, decided to see what it contained, however. When he removed the paper, the box exploded with such force that the entire building shook. Doors were ripped off their hinges, nails were pushed out of walls, furniture was broken apart, and thick smoke choked everyone inside. Tim Sullivan, a city building inspector who worked in a nearby office remembered, "I've seen a lot of buildings demolished and heard explosions as well. This was fairly potent, like a mortar shell."[16]

Americans were already on edge because of the bombing of the Murrah federal building in Oklahoma City just five days before. Now, office workers panicked and rushed into the streets. Laticia Cortez, a consultant at the nearby California

Department of Education, remembered, "They were just almost running in circles. They didn't know what it was. One woman came into our parking lot hysterically crying that there was a package and it just exploded in her boss's face."[17]

Murray, who had been bending over the bomb, was killed instantly. Because of Oklahoma City, investigators believed at first that they might be looking at the work of a copycat bomber, someone who copies crimes to gain attention and cause confusion. As soon as they analyzed the debris, however, they changed their minds. It was one of the Unabomber's creations. "Based upon our preliminary assessment of some of the material at the crime scene, the Unabom task force personnel have advised me that similarities strongly indicate that this is the work of the Unabomber,"[18] said FBI agent Richard Ross.

Pictured is the interior of the California Forestry Association showing the area where Gilbert Murray opened a package bomb in April 1995 and was killed instantly.

Analyzing material found at the crime scene was of primary importance to the Unabom investigators. Although time-consuming and frustrating, it was also a vital part of the investigation and netted enormous rewards for those who knew what they were looking for. Ronay explained:

> Bombings are a very unusual kind of a crime, in that the only evidence that remains is the fragments that are left after the explosion. So that an expert in bombings, or an expert in chemistry or an expert in handwriting or DNA [deoxyribonucleic acid] needs to take the pieces, evaluate them all, and then present a total picture, filling in the gaps of what's missing. And so, a forensic laboratory is essential, certainly, in bombing investigations.[19]

CHAPTER 2

Scraps and Splinters

Processing the Unabomber's crime scenes involved an enormous amount of work for investigators and analysts who sifted through the rubble and examined the collected debris in the crime lab. Those who carried out the work included agents from the Bureau of Alcohol, Tobacco, and Firearms (ATF) and the U.S. Postal Service, who were called in to help after the second bombing. FBI agents also contributed their skills after the attack on Flight 444 in 1979. In order to increase effectiveness, in 1993 Attorney General Janet Reno ordered the formation of the Unabom Task Force. It was made up of men and women from all three organizations and at its peak included 90 to 100 agents and 45 analysts.

The task force was not called to every bombing in the United States, however. Rather, local police departments, bomb squads, and paramedics were the first to arrive on the scene when a bomb exploded or a suspicious package was found. At those sites, they set about defusing unexploded devices, rescuing the injured, establishing boundaries so that nothing would be disturbed or contaminated, and making sure that any damaged floors, walls, and ceilings were stable.

In the process, it was sometimes noted that the bombing fit the MO of the Unabomber. Perhaps the incident took place on a university campus. Perhaps the bomb had been encased in wood. Perhaps the initials FC were found on a scrap of metal among the debris. For whatever reason, Unabom investigators were notified. It then became their responsibility to gather as many clues as possible from the wreckage.

First Steps

Finding an unexploded bomb posed an extreme hazard for investigators, but it was also a potential treasure trove of information because it was the bomber's undamaged creation. Thus when they found one, they defused it in a way that left it intact, commonly with a blast of water or a small explosive charge. In the 1990s remote control robots made defusing safer and more consistent. Marty Gavin, a former member of the Chicago police department bomb squad notes, "Most people have the impression that there's actually a hands-on physical clipping of wires. We would only do that in a life-or-death situation. Most of our techniques are remote."[20]

Many communities across the United States employ bomb squads and other special investigators to deal with bomb threats or defuse explosive devices.

If a bomb had exploded, investigators set about making sense of the destruction. They first put on clean coveralls, hard hats, goggles, and protective shoes and gloves to minimize contamination from outside sources. Everyone was aware of Locard's Exchange Principle, which states that it is virtually impossible for someone to enter a crime scene without changing it in some way, perhaps shedding a hair or leaving particles of dirt from the bottom of a shoe on the carpet. Former Los Angeles police department officer Raymond E. Foster writes:

A specialized remote control robot can be used to defuse bombs in many situations that would prove too dangerous for human beings.

Crime-scene contamination can take many forms—someone may touch an object leaving their fingerprints, or inadvertently move or take evidence from the scene, perhaps by picking up fibers on their shoes. Analyzing a scene's evidence helps explain what happened, and if an item of evidence is moved or disturbed from its resting place, the analysis could be faulty. [21]

As they entered the scene, all the investigators kept a wary eye out for more unexploded bombs—secondary devices that might have been left by the bomber to kill or maim primary responders. At the same time, they began looking for evidence. This included determining where the bomb had been placed, its size and structure, and any other clues the bomber might have left behind. Prior to 1970 it was believed that no evidence could survive a bomb blast. Later, experts understood that it was possible to find a wealth of information—everything from handwriting to tool-mark impressions—on the tiny parts of the device that lay among the dust and debris.

By the Numbers

140+

The intelligence quotient (IQ) score of a genius.

"Sift Through Everything"

One of the primary tasks was to create an accurate record of the site. Thus, one investigator took notes while another took photographs of everything from a variety of angles. Photos included debris on the floor, shrapnel embedded in the walls, and holes driven into the ceiling by flying wreckage. Later such images could be used to help determine the size and power of the bomb.

Another important task was to find all the fragments of the bomb itself. Faced with only scraps and splinters, investigators and analysts had to work hard to determine which piece of wire was relevant, which twisted bit of metal was a vital clue. Chemical agents that changed color when they came in contact with splashes of fuel were sprayed on surfaces. The scene was divided into sections so that every inch could be methodically searched. Usually investigators were on their hands and knees, turning over the rubble. Detective Dan Thompson of the Milwaukee police department observed, "You've got to sift through everything, and that takes hours, just looking for a piece of wire or a tiny spring."[22]

Processing Team

The size of a crime scene investigation team depends on the size and complexity of the locale they have to process. In the case of a bombing, there must be enough members to fill the following roles:

1 Bomb disposal technician: Disarms any explosive devices.

2 Safety specialist: Ensures that the scene is structurally safe.

3 Medical examiner: Examines any human remains and determines cause of death.

4 Forensic specialist: Checks for fingerprints, chemical agents, etc.

5 Searchers/collectors: Comb the scene for evidence.

6 Logistics specialist: Gets and maintains equipment necessary for the investigation.

7 Evidence custodian: Ensures that evidence is bagged and labeled correctly.

8 Photographer: Records the scene using cameras, video cameras, etc.

9 Sketch artist: Maps the scene, including sites where evidence, bodies, etc., are found.

It is the job of crime scene investigators to thoroughly document the scene with notes and photos, and to obtain as much physical evidence as possible.

In the Unabom case, batteries, wire, and wood were important finds. So was anything that was warped and blackened as a result of intense heat and force. That indicated that it had been at the heart of the explosion, the point where the bomb had been sitting when it went off. Each piece of evidence was placed in its own bag or box and labeled. After the hand search, every scrap of debris was gathered up using shovels, rakes, brooms, buckets, and wheelbarrows, then taken to the lab for reevaluation.

In the Lab

Evidence collected from crime scenes underwent further examination at several laboratories. These included the FBI laboratory in Quantico, Virginia, and the laboratories of the ATF and the U.S. Postal Inspection Service. The latter's national forensic laboratory is located in Dulles, Virginia, with three satellite laboratories in New York, Chicago, and Memphis, Tennessee. ATF labs are located in Ammendale, Maryland; San Francisco, California; and Atlanta, Georgia. Former ATF assistant director Patrick Hynes said: "We do more bombing investigations and examination of evidence than anyone. It's something that we do better than anyone else."[23]

In the lab, analysts painstakingly reconstructed the bomb from the metal, twisted wires, blackened batteries, and wood slivers that had been found. Forensic chemist Richard Strobel put everyone's feelings into words:

> I feel like I'm confronting a jigsaw puzzle, but it's much more difficult than the normal jigsaw puzzle. Not only have the pieces been segmented into many fragments, they've also been burned, discolored, damaged beyond recognition. In some cases, the pieces aren't even there, so I have to put this jigsaw puzzle together with a very large number of handicaps.[24]

Under microscopes, everything from pieces of monofilament fishing line to the ink found on scraps of paper packaging was

This pipe bomb debris was carefully examined at the Bureau of Alcohol, Tobacco, and Firearms (ATF) crime lab in Ammendale, Maryland.

examined by technicians, looking for some unique feature that could give them a lead. They tirelessly searched through parts manuals to match the size, shape, and manufacturer of wires, switches, timers, and detonators. They used the Bomb Reference File at the FBI laboratory in an effort to link the Unabomber's design techniques to other incidents. They used instruments such as gas chromatographs and mass spectrometers to help them determine the component parts of substances such as glue and explosives. Then they consulted with experts from such places as the Dupont Explosive Company, a maker of smokeless powder, in hope of finding where such products had been sold.

Although they compiled thousands of facts, few of them were helpful. The bomber bought only common products found in most hardware stores, then removed labels that might be traceable. He sanded everything that might carry his finger-prints or DNA (genetic material, distinctive to every human being, found in blood, perspiration, and other body fluids.) Even the stamps he attached to his packages were treated in a mixture of saltwater and oil, then stuck on with household glue. "The problem is not that there are no leads; there are too many," stated ATF agent James Cavanaugh. "And Unabomber hasn't told us enough."[25]

Updating and Organizing

Due to the length of the investigation, a tremendous amount of material and information eventually accumulated from crime scenes, lab analyses, interviews with victims, and everything else related to the investigation. Because postal inspectors, FBI agents, and ATF agents did not always cooperate and share in-formation, records were often duplicated. In addition, com-puters were not common in the early 1980s, so most records were old-fashioned paper forms held in filing cabinets. They were hard to access, time-consuming to read, and difficult to compare. To ease the problem, in 1993 the Department of Defense put a massive computer system at the task force's dis-posal. This allowed them to compare huge amounts of data in a relatively short period of time, the first time that such a sys-tem had been used in a criminal investigation.

Paper files had to be transferred to the computer, howev-er, and that was a time-consuming job. Plus, to ensure that they had every bit of information available, the task force de-cided to revisit crime scenes, take more photos, and use video-tapes to capture more details. They interviewed witnesses and victims again, asking hundreds of questions of each of them. They obtained the name of every professor, student, and em-ployee of every university associated with a Unabom event. They did the same with businesses. They entered all that into the computer, too.

It took months to complete the updating, and agents were assigned to input new information as it became available. Some worked eighteen-hour days, seven days a week, neglecting their families to accomplish the task. Nevertheless, they believed the project was worthwhile. Task force member Jim Freeman said, "[The computer allowed] us to compare big bites of data on everything from the geography of the case—where the Unabomber may have lived during various years—to which universities have been targeted."[26]

Observations

As agents gained a more complete picture of the case, they were able to make important observations. For instance, they noted that no two bombs were exactly alike, inside or out. Explosive expert Ronay noted, "Almost every one of the bombs has been crafted in a unique way, so much so that to the untrained eye, they may not be related."[27]

Bomb containers differed in size, shape, and composition. Several were wooden boxes. One was a hollowed out book. One appeared to be a road hazard—a pile of boards and nails—while another seemed to be a piece of equipment attached to a can of gasoline.

Inner components differed from bomb to bomb. Pipes that contained explosives were random in size and ranged from juice cans to copper tubing. Parts were sometimes held together with rubber bands, sometimes with string or tape. Some screws were designed to be used in metal, others in wood. Clearly the bomber took what he could find from articles around his house or from some convenient junk heap. Ronay recalled, "Nothing I could see in any of these [devices] was store-bought. I called him the 'recycle bomber.'"[28]

The power and complexity of the bombs changed with time, too. Early devices were filled with smokeless powder. Later ones contained potassium chlorate mixed with aluminum, a combination that burned longer and hotter. Early end caps were wooden and blew off easily. Later caps were steel and held in place with metal pins. Early bombs were created using one pipe. In later bombs, one pipe was nested inside another so

Essentials of the Crime Lab

Most up-to-date crime labs rely heavily on two pieces of equipment: the gas chromatograph (GC) and the mass spectrometer (MS). With these, complex mixtures found at the crime scene can be analyzed and separated into their components.

The gas chromatograph is similar to a high-intensity oven. When a liquid sample of an unknown substance is placed in it, the liquid is vaporized into a gas and then sent through a coil-shaped structure lined with chemicals. The various elements in the gas move at different speeds through the structure, with small molecules traveling faster than larger ones. In the end, gas chromatography is like a race: Elements begin at the starting line but cross the finish line at different times.

After completing gas chromatography, newly separated elements are run through a mass spectrometer. There, molecules are separated according to their different masses (comparable to their weight), then counted. Numbers are then fed into a computer, which creates a graph of the number of particles with different masses. This is known as the mass spectrum of the unknown.

that gas pressure would build to a greater degree before exploding. And instead of being filled with match heads, later bombs had nails and lead weights taped to their surfaces to inflict greater injuries. "His expertise [increases] with every device, as does his threat to the public,"[29] said two unnamed investigators who worked on the case.

Patterns

Each bomb was different, but experts were able to detect similarities, even if those similarities were subtle. For instance, other bombers might make car bombs or bombs made of plastic explosive. The Unabomber always made pipe bombs—tightly sealed sections of pipe filled with explosives.

The explosive material inside the bombs was always a type that was easily acquired by an ordinary person. Smokeless powder could be collected from ammunition. Ammonium nitrate was a key ingredient in fertilizers. Sodium chlorate was found in some weed killers. Potassium chlorate was found in matches and fireworks. That meant the bomber was an amateur, not a bomb expert who had access to military devices or plastic explosives.

Except for the third bomb set on Flight 444, all of the bombs required someone else to detonate them. The lack of success of the third device had apparently discouraged the bomber from attempting the same thing again. His detonation systems were simple, utilizing no timers, sensors, or remote controls. When a package was opened or a bag lifted, a lever moved, and the initiator sparked inside.

Uniquely Crafted

The Unabomber's devices were relatively simple, but they possessed unique details. His wooden boxes were varnished and sometimes elaborately carved. At the same time, they were crudely built. His hinges were homemade. His corners were not cut and glued in approved carpenter style. "He's not a craftsman," observed former San Francisco postal inspector Don Davis. "His cuts aren't straight. They don't make right angles. He spends a lot of time; he does a lot of polishing and sanding to make it feel nice; but they don't look really craftsmanlike."[30]

The bomber was clearly a do-it-yourself individual. He constructed switches that could have been purchased readymade from stores like Radio Shack. Instead of purchasing batteries with connectors, he used solder (a mix of lead and tin) to attach his wires. Instead of buying nails, he filed pieces of wire into points. Freeman stated, "He [the bomber] has, on occasion, made and fashioned screws and other fasteners that could be purchased in a hardware store. It was clearly the intent of the bomb-maker to conceal any potential lead value from the investigator from the outset."[31]

Another unique touch was the letters "FC," which appeared on eight of his sixteen bombs. At first, the letters were punched onto an attached metal tag. Later, they were found on the pipe's metal end plugs. Investigators came to recognize the letters as the bomber's signature—his way of expressing himself and taking credit for his work.

This signature was a significant piece of the profile that investigators created in order to better understand the man they were hunting. The process of profiling—a method of identifying a perpetrator based on how he carried out his crimes—was a little-used technique when the Unabomber began his attacks in 1978. Nevertheless, it helped investigators give some shape to a killer who was as furtive as he was deadly. With coauthor Mark Olshaker, FBI profiler John Douglas wrote of his colleagues: "We've seen enough of this that we do know what makes these guys tick, even if we don't know the specific reasoning that may be going on within their twisted minds."[32]

By the Numbers

0.5%

The percent of the American population with an intelligence quotient (IQ) score of 140 or above.

CHAPTER 3

A Shadowy Profile

Profiling, also known as criminal investigative analysis or investigative psychology, was in its infancy in the 1980s, but it had already been recognized among psychiatrists and others as a valuable tool in determining an unknown perpetrator's personality, sex, age, background, and motives. They understood, for instance, that a killer who cleaned up after a murder was organized and intelligent. One who did not was disorganized and perhaps mentally ill. "The basic premise [of profiling] is that behavior reflects personality,"[33] explained retired FBI agent Gregg McCrary, a pioneer in the field.

Instructor Howard Teten introduced the concept of profiling to the FBI about 1970. Agents McCrary, Douglas, Roy Hazelwood, and Robert K. Ressler were some of the first to study it. They dedicated their lives to developing it into an accurate and worthwhile forensic tool. McCrary notes, "Early on it was just a bunch of us [FBI agents] basing our work on our investigative experience, and hopefully being right more than we were wrong."[34] To broaden their experience and hone their skills, however, they examined what perpetrators did to victims. They spent their free time interviewing prisoners. They tried to understand those prisoners' thinking and reasoning, all the while remaining as objective as possible.

"The Guy in the Background"

FBI agent John Douglas created the first Unabom profile in 1980. He was a consultant on the Atlanta Child Murders in Georgia, the BTK (Bind, Torture, Kill) murders in Wichita, Kansas, and the Yorkshire Ripper murders in England at the time. Nevertheless, when Chicago FBI agent Tom Barrett

FBI profiler Gregg McCrary, pictured in 2001, was one of the first agents to learn the technique of criminal profiling in the 1970s.

asked for his help, Douglas took the time to review the four bombings that had taken place and combine the facts with observations about bombers in general to come up with his description of the Unabomber.

Aware that most bombers were men, Douglas postulated that the Unabomber was male. He was probably in his late twenties or early thirties and was likely Caucasian. Again, most

FBI agent John Douglas created the first Unabom profile in 1980. Over time and more bombings, other agents added to Douglas's original profile.

bombers fit this description. His attacks were likely triggered by some traumatic event such as abuse or an insult that he had brooded over for a long time. Douglas and Olshaker wrote, "There can be many different kinds of triggers, but the ones we've uncovered most often . . . are a loss of job and the end of a relationship with a significant other person. Sometimes those two things will come together. . . . We had no real idea what the Unabomber's initial trigger might have been, but we were sure there was something."[35]

Douglas pointed out that the bomber would not look like a wild-eyed maniac. Rather, because he was capable of organizing, planning, and avoiding detection, he probably looked ordinary, like everyone's next-door neighbor. He probably appeared to be a law-abiding person and had no criminal record. He would not have an outgoing personality. He would have trouble trusting people and would have few friends. Douglas stated, "He'd be the type of person who might hold a night job because he felt more comfortable when there weren't a lot of people around. It was unlikely he belonged to any sort of organized political group or movement, but if he did, he would be the guy in the background, not a demonstrator type."[36]

Adjustments and Disagreements

With time and more bombings, other profilers like FBI agents William Tafoya and Mary Ellen O'Toole added to and fine-tuned the original Unabom profile. The fact that the bomber regularly targeted universities around the country convinced them that he had been on at least one campus for a period of time. Perhaps he was a professor or a researcher who was holding a grudge. Douglas believed that "there was a good chance that he considered himself an innovative

Becoming a Profiler

Job Description:
Criminal profilers rely on psychology and experience in criminology to create a portrait of an unknown perpetrator. They perform crime scene analyses, read police reports, and research earlier cases for patterns of criminal behavior.

Education:
Aspiring profilers must earn a four-year degree in behavioral science, criminology, sociology, criminal justice, or a related field from an accredited college or university. They must also gain experience in crime prevention and pass the Profiling General Knowledge Exam (PGKE), which tests their knowledge of forensic science, victimology, crime scene analysis, criminal profiling, expert testimony, and professional ethics.

Personal Qualifications:
An aspiring profiler must have a logical and analytical approach to work, an open mind, highly developed observational skills, and the willingness to try to understand and think like an offender.

Salary:
A criminal profiler can earn a salary that ranges from $40,000 to more than $70,000 annually.

intellectual pioneer who was bitter because he hadn't made tenure or been given due credit for his discoveries."[37]

The conviction that the bomber was an academic was reinforced by evidence that he knew how to lull educators' suspicions when an odd package came their way. He used the return addresses of fellow professors who might be expected to communicate with each other. He disguised two of the bombs as books, something an educator might expect to receive.

Other investigators disputed the conclusion that the bomber was a scholar, however. They felt that because he targeted airlines, he was probably a blue-collar worker, possibly

While much evidence in the Unabomb case seemed to point to the fact that the bomber was a scholar or university professor, still other evidence pointed to his being a mechanic or other skilled labor professional.

a mechanic of some kind. Perhaps he had learned his skills while working for one of the airlines or for an aircraft manufacturer. Perhaps he worked there still. Douglas observed, "Analysis of his techniques in creating the bombs prompted some of the experts to insist that . . . that was the only way he would have picked up these skills."[38] During the course of the investigation, almost every mechanic who had worked in the airline industry since the late 1960s was interviewed and/or investigated, but the bomber was not found.

Symbols

As profiling continued to develop, the profilers began analyzing the Unabomber's crimes from different perspectives. In addition to offender profiling, they used victim profiling— analysis of the lives of the victims—to gain insight into his movements, motives, intent, and fantasies. Learning about the victims might provide clues to the bomber's past, because it was likely that he had come in contact with them at some point. Perhaps he had been in a class with one of them. Perhaps he had purchased something from a company for which they worked.

Everyone and everything connected with the victims was identified and scrutinized. Other than the fact that most could be linked in some way with technology, computers, airlines, or the environment, however, there appeared to be nothing that gave new insights into the bomber's life and character. "I think the victims are symbols, not individuals this person knows and dislikes,"[39] Fischer said.

Even if the victims were merely symbols, the bomber had sent some of his bombs to specific people, and their names had come from somewhere. Profilers believed that the bomber had gotten them from magazines, scientific journals, or outdated reference books at his local library. The fact that the bomber's information was not always up-to-date supported that premise. For instance, the sixth bomb was mailed to Patrick Fischer at Pennsylvania State University, but Fischer had left that university two years before. The bomb sent to the California Forestry

Association in 1995 was addressed to William Dennison, who had given up his post as its president a year earlier.

Investigators even believed they had identified one of the magazines from which the bomber got his information. A 1994 copy of the *Earth First! Journal*, a radical environmentalist journal, erroneously stated that the public relations firm Burson-Marsteller had represented the Exxon Corporation after their tanker, the *Valdez*, spilled oil in Alaska's Prince William Sound in 1989. Thomas Mosser had been vice president of Burson-Marsteller at the time of the spill. In fact, Burson-Marsteller had not represented Exxon, but if the Unabomber had read the article, it would have explained why he had targeted Mosser.

"A Rigid Personality"

Victim profiling gave investigators only limited insight into the bomber's mind and motivations. Crime scene profiling—analyzing his crime scenes and the evidence found there— better helped them determine how he planned and executed his crimes. The fact that he often placed his devices in plain sight but was never seen, for instance, indicated that he was smart enough to figure out the best times to come and go without notice. He knew how to blend into a crowd. The fact that his bombs were made of common everyday items meant that he knew how to avoid detection. The fact that he never left DNA or fingerprints meant that he was knowledgeable about forensics.

Unexploded devices that were found at some scenes gave profilers their best insights into his personality. For instance, he placed more than enough stamps on his parcels, and most of the stamps had been issued years before. This indicated that he avoided contact with post office employees who might later identify him. His hand-carved boxes that were carefully painted black on the inside revealed an obsession with details. Numbers found on various parts of the bombs revealed that he took them apart and put them back together again, perhaps several times. Ronay observed, "It's not just that he's creating some-

Pairings

In profiling the Unabomber, investigators noticed that he often planned and executed his crimes in pairs. The significance of the pairing was puzzling, however, as journalists Nancy Gibbs, Richard Lacayo, Lance Morrow, Jill Smolowe, and David Van Biema note in their book Mad Genius: The Odyssey, Pursuit, and Capture of the Unabomber Suspect:

With the twin bombings in 1993, investigators began to see new patterns. The Unabomber had set off bombs two months apart in 1982; in 1985 there had been two pairs of bombs that went off within a month of each other. . . .

There were other peculiar pairings. Two times, he had struck Cory Hall at Berkeley. Twice he had selected airline personnel as his targets. Twice he had struck in Salt Lake City. His list of victims included two people who owned computer stores, two computer engineers, two electrical scientists, two graduate students. Two Fischers had been listed on his parcels. Two bombs had struck at Boeing targets. And twice the bomber had used the names of Sacramento professors for the return addresses.

But what, if anything, did it all add up to?

Nancy Gibbs, Richard Lacayo, Lance Morrow, Jill Smolowe, and David Van Biema, *Mad Genius: The Odyssey, Pursuit, and Capture of the Unabomber Suspect.* New York: Warner, 1996, pp. 90–91.

thing carefully. He's played with it for a while. He marks things with numbers so he can put them together again right."[40]

If the bomber was careful, methodical, and detail oriented when it came to his devices, profilers believed he would be particular about other things, too. His home might be cluttered, but his workspace would be orderly. He would likely keep journals in which he recorded everything he did. Douglas said, "He has a rigid personality. You have to be a rigid personality to do what he does. Everything in its place. In order."[41]

The Personal Touch

Some of the most interesting information profilers gained about the devices came from the bomber's signature—the personal touch on his bombs that satisfied his creative sense. There were two signatures, the first being the letters FC. Profilers speculated long and hard over their meaning. Many believed they stood for an obscene phrase relating to computers. Others thought they might have a religious message.

The bomber's second signature was his obsession with wood. He used wood to craft his boxes. He unnecessarily covered some of his devices with wood. He used wooden dowels as part of his detonation system. He used wooden caps to plug the ends of his pipe bombs, even though metal would have been more practical.

The bomber not only used wood, he referred to it in a variety of ways. Some references were obvious, like the fact that he chose names with the word "wood" in them —Percy Wood and LeRoy Wood Bearnson—when addressing his packages. Some were more subtle. For instance, Wood lived in Lake Forest, Illinois. Mosser lived on Aspen Drive. Investigators noted that the words "forest," "moss," and "aspen" all had connections to wood. The book *Ice Brothers* was published by Arbor House. Arbors are leafy bowers formed by tree branches. Arbor House's logo was a leaf. Finally, many of the bombs were mailed from Oakland, California, named for the oak trees that grow on the hills.

There were the extremely subtle allusions, too, that might easily have been overlooked. The bomber used green ink to address at least one of his packages—green being the color of trees. In at least one of his bombs he used barium nitrate, a type of explosive. Former postal inspector Tony Muljat, who pursued the bomber for more than ten years, explained, "[It was] fireworks powder, just used to color the smoke *green*."[42]

Investigators were convinced that the wood theme was associated with the bomber's hatred of technology, but the knowledge did not lead them to a specific person.

Comfort Zone

At the same time investigators tried to learn more about the bomber's reasoning from his victims and his crime scenes, they hoped that geographic profiling would help lead them to his door. The concept of geographic profiling is based on the premise that everyone has a mental map—an image of their surroundings—that forms as a result of their personal experiences. Because criminals, like everyone else, are most comfortable acting within the boundary of their mental map, they are likely to gravitate there to commit their crimes.

If that conclusion held true, the bomber appeared to be familiar with a wide variety of locales. His devices had been mailed to or from, or placed in, the Chicago area; Nashville, Tennessee; New Haven, Connecticut; Salt Lake City, Utah; Ann Arbor, Michigan; and northern California. Some locales seemed more important than others, however. For instance, several of the early devices originated in the Chicago area. That seemed to indicate that the bomber might have grown up there.

All of the later bombs had been postmarked Sacramento, Oakland, and San Francisco. That seemed to be a sign that the bomber had moved to California. It was unlikely that he lived in one of those cities, however, because testing his devices would certainly have drawn unwanted attention from his neighbors. Thus, they postulated he

Investigators wondered if the Ice Brothers *book, which was used in the first bombing, was a deliberate choice—to be viewed as a clue—or just a random book used by the Unabomber.*

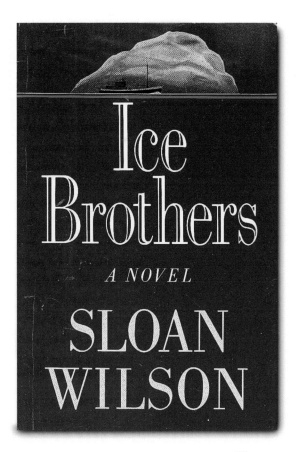

lived in a more rural part of northern California, but near enough to be able to get to a city to mail his bombs in anonymity.

Who Is the Unabomber?

With a profile in place and many leads to follow, the task force investigated thousands of suspects over eighteen years. These ranged from mechanics to environmental activists. Most were quickly eliminated. Others remained under scrutiny for longer periods of time.

Some of the earliest suspects were college students at Northwestern University who belonged to a Dungeons & Dragons club. The fantasy role-playing game had received negative publicity for its alleged championing of devil worship, witchcraft, suicide, and murder. Some investigators believed that players in the club could have built and planted the first, amateurish bombs. A thorough check by law enforcement, however, was enough to quickly clear the students of any involvement in the Unabom incidents.

Two other suspects were Californian James William Kilgore and Pennsylvanian Leo Burt. Kilgore had been a fugitive since 1975 when, as a member of the paramilitary Symbionese Liberation Army, he had helped commit a string of terrorist acts in California that included pipe bombings. Burt, a former marine, had been a fugitive since 1970 when he had fled after a bombing at the University of Wisconsin Army Mathematics Research Center in Madison, Wisconsin. He was a critic of bureaucracy, opposed technology, and resembled the eyewitness sketch of the Unabomber.

Investigators checked out both men and eventually eliminated them as suspects, primarily because they were not secretive loners that the Unabomber was believed to be. Davis stated, "We looked at Burt and Kilgore a few years ago—we never found any reason to believe it was either of those folks."[43]

More Suspects

Hundreds of other suspects cropped up over the years. In early 1995 some of the task force believed their man might be

An Art Form

Even if they use the same components in their bombs, few serial bombers make their devices the same way. Each will have his own signature—a special style or technique— as author David Fisher points out in his book Hard Evidence:

For some bomb makers, making a bomb is an art form, and their productions, like those of great artists, bear their unmistakable handiwork. Their signature. No matter what subject [artist Vincent] van Gogh painted, his style was unique and identifiable. . . . The same was true of . . . the killer known as Unabomber, whose deadly craftsmanship . . . plagued law enforcement for more than a decade.

"For most of my career I never used the word 'signature,'" [FBI explosive expert] Fred Smith remembered. "But as time moved on, I realized there truly are signatures in bomb making. I may make the most reliable bomb in the world, but I only know how to make it one way. Well, when a bomb has four or eight, whatever, points of construction that are the same as other bombs, it's appropriate to conclude that the same person made all those bombs. . . . To me, that's a signature."

The [FBI] lab introduced the concept that bombs could be linked by a signature in the early 1980s, and after initial resistance the courts have accepted signatures as evidence. A signature can be the construction, the design of the circuitry, the materials used, including the explosive, even the method used to deliver the bomb.

David Fisher, *Hard Evidence.* New York: Simon & Schuster, 1995, p. 85.

Stephen Dunifer, founder of Free Radio Berkeley, an unlicensed radio station in the San Francisco Bay area. Dunifer, who proved to be innocent, spent significant amounts of time in his shop, working with wood and electronics. Another person of interest was a university worker who was critical of technology and whose initials were FC. "He sure looked good," remembered Ronay. "But he was out of the country at some points and there were other things that made it clear he couldn't possibly have done it."[44]

The task force also checked out several men whose first names were Robert and whose last names began with the letter V. That line of investigation was based on a note found attached to one of the 1982 bombs and a tip from Northwestern University professor Donald Saari. The note read, "Wu—it works! I told you it would. R.V."[45] When Saari read a copy of the note, he thought he remembered a student with the name "Robert V" asking him to help publish an antitechnology paper in 1977 or 1978. Saari remembered the student had been angry when he did not get the help he expected and threatened to get even. Despite Saari's tip, however, the lead came to nothing.

For a time investigators believed that the Unabomber might have mistakenly left the note "Wu—it works!" on the bomb. Over time, however, they understood him better and realized that the note had been deliberately placed for them to find. Why he did it, no one knew for sure. Perhaps he wanted to communicate with them. Perhaps the note was a taunt. No matter which, it was plain to see that he arrogantly believed he could take such an obvious step without being caught.

His arrogance became even clearer in 1995 after he mailed out a lengthy document—his manifesto—expressing his views on technology and modern American society. Ironically, that rambling, opinionated message proved more powerful than any hard evidence or eyewitness report: It eventually provided investigators with the key to bringing him to justice. "His fatal mistake was the manifesto," said former FBI agent James Esposito. "That was his undoing. I knew as soon as I saw it that it was going to lead to his identification."[46]

CHAPTER 4

The Bomber's Words

The Unabomber did not communicate extensively with the outside world before 1993. When he did, he always did so through writing. His messages were short and were usually "red herrings"—left deliberately to confuse and sidetrack the investigation.

As the years passed his confidence and daring seemed to grow. He wrote more often and at greater length, openly expressing his feelings. From these communications investigators gained a much clearer picture of his purpose and motivation. They also became more confident that his words would one day lead them to his hiding place. Fox said of the bomber in 1995, "He's feeling invincible, that he's superior to law enforcement and can forever outsmart the police. Hopefully that's what will be his downfall."[47]

Red Herrings

The Unabomber was notorious for his short written clues that seemed revealing but went nowhere. For instance, when investigators tried to track down the name "Enoch Fischer," the sender of the letter to Wood in June 1980, they discovered it was fictitious. So was Fischer's address, which turned out to be a vacant lot in Ravenswood, a neighborhood in the Chicago metro area.

The message "Wu—It works!" was another example of a promising clue that fizzled. When investigators were unable to connect the message to anyone named Wu, they decided the sentence might be some type of code. They consulted everyone from scholars to code experts in an attempt to decipher it, all without success. Bill Foley of the UC Berkeley

Becoming a Forensic Document Examiner

Job Description:
Forensic document examiners make scientific examinations, comparisons, and analyses of documents for the purpose of establishing authenticity, accuracy, identity of the author, etc. They also prepare reports and testify as expert witnesses in courts of law.

Education:
Aspiring document examiners must earn a bachelor of science degree from an accredited college or university. They must then go on to complete a two-year full-time training program in forensic document examination in a recognized forensic laboratory under the guidance of an experienced questioned document examiner. Certification by the American Board of Forensic Document Examiners is recommended.

Personal Qualifications:
Forensic document examiners must have excellent eyesight to notice fine details that may be inconspicuous to others. They must also be patient, meticulous, and thorough in their study of documents.

Salary:
A forensic document examiner can earn a salary that ranges from $30,000 to more than $70,000 annually.

police department remembered, "We [ran] that 'Wu' thing every which way to Sunday. We [interviewed] people with that name. We tried to figure out if it was left by the bomber, or if it was left by someone else. We ran all this down and really came up with nothing."[48]

The red herrings continued even after the bomber began his letter writing campaign in the 1990s. In a long, rambling letter to the *New York Times* in April 1995, he alluded to the fact that he was getting tired of "searching the Sierras for a place isolated enough to test a bomb."[49] Assuming the word "Sierras" referred to the Sierra Nevada mountain range in California, investigators thoroughly searched the region in hope of finding evidence that he had tested his devices there. Despite the effort, they found nothing. They finally concluded that the reference was just another false lead, deliberately planted because the bomber enjoyed mocking their failure. He felt so superior and confident of his abilities that he took the unnecessary risk of leaving clues simply to satisfy his ego. Fox observed, "He gets a tremendous sense of pride by outsmarting everyone."[50]

Direct Communication

In 1993 the bomber became more communicative as he began writing to various individuals throughout the United States. On June 24 Warren Hoge, an assistant managing editor of the *New York Times*, received a letter mailed from Sacramento announcing that a "newsworthy event" would soon take place. The letter was late arriving, however, and the event had already occurred. That day David Gelernter had been the victim of a bombing attributed to the Unabomber. Two days before, Charles Epstein had been seriously wounded in a similar blast.

It was the first concrete bit of information ever received from the bomber. And the letter contained more. The bomber went on to state that "FC"—Freedom Club—was an anarchist group. In addition, he provided an identifying number—553-25-4394—that he said could be used to "ensure the authenticity of any future communication from us."[51]

The 1993 World Trade Center bombing, pictured, generated big headlines, perhaps prompting a jealous Unabomber to write letters to the media after nearly fifteen years without contact.

The letter was a breakthrough, but investigators wondered why the bomber had decided to speak out after fifteen years of virtual silence. From what they knew of his arrogance, they guessed that he was jealous. Just four months before, on February 26, a group of terrorists had captured the world's attention by planting a car bomb under the World Trade Center in New York City. They had killed 6 people and injured 1,042 in an attempt to collapse the twin towers that were symbols of American prosperity and power. The attack had definitely drawn the spotlight from the Unabomber. Undoubtedly, he had decided to grab it back with the letter and the attacks on Gelernter and Epstein.

Fresh Clues

Regardless of his motives, investigators now had new information to work on. The number 553-25-4394 was in the format used by the Social Security Administration, so they checked those records. They led to a paroled ex-convict in his twenties, living in California. The man had been in prison when the bombings occurred, so he was not the Unabomber. Oddly enough, though, he had a tattoo on his arm that said "Pure Wood." If the Unabomber had chosen the number at random, it was a strange coincidence. If he had met the convict and somehow obtained his social security number in the past, investigators guessed that he was again taunting them with clues that seemed promising but led nowhere.

The number proved disappointing, but there was still another clue to follow. As they examined the paper on which the letter to Hoge was written, investigators saw a faint impression of the words "Call Nathan R Wed 7 P.M."[52] It was as if the bomber had pressed down while writing on the top sheet of a stack of paper and without realizing it, left impressions on the paper below.

Investigators set out to discover who Nathan R was. From the message, it appeared that the bomber had communicated with him in the recent past, so they searched phone books and driver's license records nationwide. Over ten thousand individuals named Nathan with a middle or last initial "R" were identified and interviewed, but no connection to the bomber was made.

Taunts and Insults

Almost two years passed before the bomber was heard from again. Then on April 19, 1995, antigovernment militants Timothy McVeigh and Terry Nichols left a car bomb in front of the Murrah federal building in Oklahoma City. When it exploded, the bomb destroyed the nine-story building and took

Within days of the April 19, 1995, bombing of the Murrah federal building in the Oklahoma City bombing, pictured, the Unabomber contacted the New York Times, *revealing information about some of his past killings.*

the lives of 168 people, many of them children. All eyes turned to Oklahoma City, as Americans mourned what was called "the most devastating terrorist event of recent history, the greatest on U.S. soil."[53]

With his crimes again pushed from the spotlight, the Unabomber made another bid for attention. He began sending letters to various people just a week later. Criminologist Fox opined, "When there are such big headlines describing the Oklahoma City explosion as 'the largest bombing of its kind,' it is . . . enough to make another bomber feel a little envious."[54]

Boasting and Threats

The Unabomber combined boasting and threats in his April 24, 1995, letter to New York Times *editor William Hoge. The following excerpt from that letter can be found in John Douglas and Mark Olshaker's* Unabomber: On the Trail of America's Most-Wanted Serial Killer:

Since we no longer have to confine the explosive in a pipe, we are now free of limitations on the size and shape of our bombs. We are pretty sure we know how to increase the power of our explosives . . . so we expect to be able to pack deadly bombs into ever smaller, lighter, and more harmless looking packages. On the other hand, we believe we will be able to make bombs much bigger than any we've made before. With a briefcase-full or a suitcase-full, we should be able to blow out the walls of substantial buildings.

Clearly we are in a position to do a great deal of damage. And it doesn't appear that the FBI is going to catch us any time soon.

The FBI is a joke.

Quoted in John Douglas and Mark Olshaker, *Unabomber: On the Trail of America's Most-Wanted Serial Killer.* New York: Pocket Books, 1996, p. 184.

On April 24, 1995, two Nobel Prize winners, geneticists Phillip Sharp of the Massachusetts Institute of Technology and Richard Roberts of New England Biolabs in Massachusetts, each received threatening letters. In them the bomber warned, "It would be beneficial to your health to stop your research in genetics."[55] Both men had done groundbreaking work that was fundamental to biotechnology.

Gelernter also received a taunting letter from the bomber on April 24. It read: "People with advanced degrees aren't as smart as they think they are. If you'd had any brains you would have realized that there are a lot of people out there who resent bitterly the way techno-nerds like you are changing the world and you wouldn't have been dumb enough to open an unexpected package from an unknown source."[56]

Further Revelations

The bomber sent a second letter to the *New York Times* on April 24 as well. As he had promised in 1993, he included the identifying number that guaranteed the letter's authenticity. He then surprised everyone by revealing information that investigators had been waiting years to hear. First, he took credit for killing Mosser. He explained that Mosser's firm, Burson-Marsteller, had not only "helped Exxon clean up its public image after the Exxon Valdez incident,"[57] it was trying to manipulate people's attitudes, which the bomber opposed.

Next, the bomber cleared up any confusion over his choice of targets. He wrote: "We have nothing against universities or scholars as such. All the university people we have attacked have been specialists in technical fields. . . . The people we are out to get are the scientists and engineers, especially in critical fields like computers and genetics."[58]

He also explained his goals—to draw attention to the evils of technology, to attract supporters, and through them to eventually destroy modern society.

We call ourselves anarchists because we would like, ideally, to break down all society into very small, completely autonomous [independent] units. Regrettably, we don't see any clear road to this goal, so we leave it to the indefinite future. Our more immediate goal, which we think may be attainable at some time during the next several decades, is the destruction of the worldwide industrial system.[59]

The Demand

At the end of the letter the bomber stated that he was growing tired of making bombs and instead wanted to "propagate [spread] ideas." "We offer a bargain," he wrote. "We have a long article, between 29,000 and 37,000 words, that we want to have published."[60]

The bomber's publisher of choice was the *New York Times*, although he would allow the article to be printed in *Time*, *Newsweek*, or some other nationally distributed periodical. *Penthouse*, a well-known men's magazine, did not measure up to his standards. When *Penthouse* publisher Robert Guccione stated his willingness to print the manuscript, the bomber decreed that if he were the only one to do so, he would stage one additional bombing.

The bomber's demand included the right to have follow-up articles published for the next three years. "If you can get it published according to our requirements we will permanently desist from [stop] our terrorist activities," he promised. But he was quick to make a distinction between terrorist activities and sabotage—destruction of property without harming human beings. "The promise we offer is to desist from terrorism," he wrote. "We reserve the right to engage in sabotage."[61]

The Manifesto

Before anyone had time to make a decision about the bomber's article, he mailed copies of it to both the *Times* and the *Washington Post*. Entitled "Industrial Society and its Future," it was fifty-six pages long, included eleven pages of footnotes, and advocated revolution against the industrial system. "The technophiles [technology lovers] are taking us all on an utterly reckless ride into the unknown. Many people understand something of what technological progress is doing to us yet take a passive attitude toward it because they think it is inevitable. But we (FC) don't think it is inevitable. We think it can be stopped."[62]

The bomber pointed out that modern industrial society with its laws, public education systems, media influence, and so forth, pressured individuals to conform. That led to a loss of personal freedom as well as a sense of powerlessness, defeat, guilt, and depression. "Since the beginning of civilization, organized societies have had to put pressures on human beings for the sake of the functioning of the social organism,"[63] he wrote.

The bomber believed, however, that as technology continued to advance, human beings would eventually be totally controlled by machines or by a tiny elite group who used technology for their own purposes. Reforming the system would only bring a partial and/or temporary fix. The real solution was revolution, which would totally destroy modern society. Humankind would then be forced to turn back to nature where they would find true meaning in life. He wrote, "To feed themselves they must be peasants or herdsmen or fishermen or hunters, etc. And, generally speaking, local autonomy [independence] should tend to increase, because lack of advanced technology and rapid communications will limit the capacity of governments or other large organizations to control local communities."[64]

By the Numbers

$30,000 – $40,000

The cost of printing the Unabomber Manifesto.

Between the Lines

More important than what the manifesto said was what it revealed about the bomber. Its academic tone and format, similar to a thesis with introduction, conclusion, and footnotes, supported the profilers' beliefs that he was intelligent and well educated. He was comfortable when he was writing, but obsessive, as his carefully defined words and numbered paragraphs indicated.

The manifesto's themes revealed that he experienced feelings of powerlessness, alienation, and depression. References such as "One of the most important means by which our society socializes children is by making them feel ashamed of behavior or speech that is contrary to society's expectations"[65] revealed that he looked back on his childhood as unhappy. Other phrases such as "[The technophiles say] 'we will conquer famine, eliminate psychological suffering, making everyone happy and healthy.' Yeah, sure."[66] proclaimed his feelings of superiority.

Profilers could detect a great deal of anger in the manifesto as well. With such rage, they felt certain he would not keep his promise to stop bombing even if his work was published. Undoubtedly, more deadly attacks would occur if he was not caught.

The Debate

With the arrival of the manifesto, debate heated up over whether or not it should be published. The bomber's demand was a form of blackmail, and publishing it, even if it saved lives, was against everyone's principles. "To print this manuscript, even a part of it, is a terrible precedent. It's like paying off hijackers. If a person knows they can extort this kind of thing out of the press, where will it stop?"[67] asked ethicist Michael Josephson.

Others pointed out that publishing would give the public a chance to read his writing. Someone might recognize his style, his opinions, or even a turn of phrase or a unique expression. Dartmouth journalism professor Ronald Green stated, "This individual has proven himself to be very dangerous. If there's even a reasonable chance that publishing this article could put an end to his career, then I think the publishers of the *New York Times* and the *Washington Post* should take that chance."[68]

Task force member Freeman supported the latter point of view. The FBI had originally believed that information about the Unabomber should be kept private for fear that publicity would fuel his ego, increase the number of bombings, or cause him to change his MO. They were also afraid that cooperating with a terrorist would lead other terrorists to expect similar treatment. But by 1994 they were desperate to get new leads. FBI agent Rick Smith remembered, "Jim Freeman had a lot to do with the publishing of that manuscript. He was able to encourage others to support his position. And he was able then to convince headquarters to do it, convince Department of Justice (and Janet Reno) to do it. He was a real key guy and very effective."[69]

An Epic-Length Attack on Technology

After weeks of debate, on September 13, 1995, Reno, FBI director Louis Freeh, and publishers Arthur Sulzberger Jr. of the *Times* and Donald E. Graham of the *Post* agreed that the manifesto would be published. Because the *Post* had the ability to distribute the manifesto as a separate section of its daily paper, it and the *Times* joined forces and split the cost of publishing. The resulting eight-page insert came out on September 19, 1995. Over eight hundred fifty thousand copies were printed. In addition, entertainment and media giant Time Warner

The Unabomber's thirty-five thousand-word manifesto was published in a special section of The Washington Post *on September 19, 1995.*

posted a copy on the Internet, prompting *Time* magazine journalist Nancy Gibbs and others to point out that it was "the first epic-length attack on technology to be sent everywhere on a computer network."[70]

As newspapers flew off the stands, discussion over the correctness of the decision continued. "It was a huge mistake," opined Jane Kirtley, executive director of the Reporters' Committee for Freedom of the Press. On the other hand, President Bill Clinton approved the move. "I applaud them. They acted in a good and brave way."[71]

Revolutionary or Boring?

Once the Unabom manifesto was printed in the Washington Post, *everyone realized that its length and scholarly style would discourage customers from buying it. Even so, as Robert Graysmith reports in his book* Unabomber: A Desire to Kill, *one northern California press took a chance and published the article in book form:*

On October 13 [1995], a small Berkeley publisher, Jolly Roger Press, normally known for printing chess books, brought UNABOM's anti-technology manifesto out in a $9.95 paperback. Publisher Kristan Lawson typed the manuscript into his computer in one sitting while perched on the edge of his bed. Lawson sold three thousand copies of the eleven-thousand-print run.

"To be perfectly honest," he said of his bestseller, "it's boring. It's not even wildly revolutionary. I've read much more inflammatory stuff. I think it's obvious (the Unabomber) was once a member of some left-wing group, and some girl in it spurned [rejected] him."

Robert Graysmith, *Unabomber: A Desire to Kill.* Washington, DC: Regnery, 1997, p. 361.

Whether right or wrong, publication netted results. The FBI's tip line was flooded with thousands of calls. And in Schenectady, New York, David Kaczynski read the manifesto repeatedly and tried to convince himself that his brother Theodore could not be its author. He remembers, "It wasn't possible to read about the bombings—the unsuspecting victims, the horrified and grieving families—and not feel a sudden twinge of pity. I wondered what it must feel like to be 'struck by lightning,' to feel one's whole universe shift and teeter as a result of some seemingly random violence. Unfortunately for me, I was soon to find out."[72]

CHAPTER 5

The Montana Hermit

When David Kaczynski approached authorities with suspicions about his brother, the Unabom investigation took a gigantic leap forward. The task force realized almost immediately that the quiet man from Schenectady had, in just a few months, been able to go further toward identifying the elusive killer than they had been able to in eighteen years. Attorney Anthony Bisceglie, who represented David in 1995, said, "But for David, this case would not have been solved."[73]

The Good Man

The decision to inform on his brother had not been easy for David, whose life revolved around helping others. A college graduate from Columbia University, he spent his days counseling troubled teens and caring for his elderly mother. He and his wife Linda were known for their generosity. "They're very sweet, extremely polite and truthful people," said neighbor Mary Ann Welch. "They're the kind of neighbors who lend you their car when yours is in the shop, who offer their gardening tools."[74]

Linda had been the first to read the manifesto in the *Post* and remark on the fact that it sounded like David's brother, Theodore, whom everyone called Ted. At her insistence, David read it, too. He was dismayed to discover that the ideas and language sounded familiar. One sentence in particular stood out. Instead of using the common form of the proverb "You can't have your cake and eat it, too," the writer of the manifesto stated, "You can't eat your cake and have it, too."[75] David realized that he and Ted had heard their mother invert the phrase in just the same way all the years they had been growing up.

As David gave the matter more thought, he noted other similarities between Ted and the Unabomber. Ted had criticized scientists, corporations, and bureaucrats in the past. The manifesto echoed those criticisms. Ted was adept at woodcarving; David remembered he had once made an intricately carved sewing box for a family friend and a cylindrical box for his mother Wanda. The Unabomber was known for housing his bombs in wooden boxes. Ted had grown up in Chicago, studied in Michigan, and taught in Berkeley, all places where bombings had occurred. David recalled, "I began to feel chilled. I started getting a crushing sense of depression. . . . I looked up at Linda and said, 'There might be a 50-50 chance Ted wrote the manifesto.'"[76]

It was a tip from David Kaczynski, pictured, that led to the capture of the Unabomber, now known to be Ted Kaczynski, David's brother.

A Brilliant Start

David's fear was intensified because of the love and admiration he had for his older brother. Born in Chicago in 1942, Ted was a brilliant student with an intelligence quotient (IQ) of a genius. He skipped two grades in school, graduated from high school as a National Merit Scholarship finalist, and entered Harvard University in 1958 when he was only sixteen. After graduation from Harvard in 1962, he went on to get his masters degree in mathematics at the University of Michigan. He also earned his PhD in a branch of complex analysis known as geometric function theory, becoming one of only a dozen people in the country who knew and understood it. "He did not make mistakes," said George Piranian, who taught a course in advanced function theory during Ted's second year at Michigan. Ted had impressed him by solving a complex problem that had baffled Piranian and other professors. "He was very persistent in his work. If a problem was hard, he worked harder. He was easily the top student, or one of the top."[77]

In 1967 Ted added to his impressive achievements by joining the faculty of the University of California at Berkeley as an assistant professor of mathematics. Calvin Moore, vice chair

Theodore Kaczynski was a brilliant student, having entered the prestigious Harvard University at the age of sixteen.

THEODORE JOHN KACZYNSKI

Born: May 22, 1942 in Chicago, Ill. Prepared at Evergreen Park H.S., Evergreen Park, Ill. Home Address: 9209 Lawndale, Evergreen Park, Ill. Field of Concentration: Mathematics. Scholarships and Prizes: Harvard College Scholarship.

Private Thoughts

Although extremely private, the Unabomber freely expressed his innermost thoughts in the pages of his journals. Lincoln, Montana, resident Chris Waits was present when those journals were found and included an excerpt from one of them in his book Unabomber: The Secret Life of Ted Kaczynski, *coauthored with Dave Shors:*

In high school and college, I often became terribly angry at someone, or hated someone, but as a matter of prudence, I could not express that anger or hatred openly. I would therefore indulge in fantasies of dire revenge. However, I never attempted to put any such fantasies into effect, because I was too strongly conditioned by my early training. . . . To be more precise: I could not have committed a crime of revenge, even a relatively minor crime, because my fear of being caught and punished was all out of proportion to the actual danger of being caught. . . . This was very frustrating and humiliating. Therefore I became more and more determined that some day I would actually take revenge on some of the people I hated.

Quoted in Chris Waits and Dave Shors, *Unabomber: The Secret Life of Ted Kaczynski.* Helena, MT: Farcountry, 1999, p. 268.

of the department in 1968, remembered that everyone was impressed with the young man's thesis and record of publications. Moore believed "[Kaczynski] could have advanced up the ranks and been a senior member of the faculty."[78]

In 1969, however, Ted resigned without an explanation. John W. Addison, former chair of the math department, remembered that some of his colleagues tried and failed to convince the young professor to stay. Addison wrote, "He said he was going to give up mathematics and wasn't sure what he was going to do. He was very calm and relaxed about it on the outside. We tried to persuade him to reconsider, but our presentation had no apparent effect."[79]

Troubled Genius

David knew what Ted intended to do when he left Berkeley. He hoped to buy land in Canada and escape from the confines of modern society. This was because, although Ted was successful academically, he was a failure socially. In elementary school he felt uncomfortable around other children, seeing them as stupid or troublemakers. Rather than playing, he would retreat to his room and read mathematics and chemistry books. He felt awkward around adults, too. Physican LeRoy Weinberg, a former Kaczynski neighbor, recalled, "I would see him coming in the alley. He'd always walk by without saying hello. Just nothing. Ted is a brilliant boy, but he was most unsociable. . . . This kid didn't play. No, no. He was an old man before his time."[80]

In high school Ted was good-looking and interested in girls but was too shy to relate well with them. He later recalled, "My attempts to make advances to girls had such humiliating results that for many years afterward, even until after the age of 30, I found it excruciatingly difficult—almost impossible—to make advances to women. . . . At the age of 19 to 20, I had a girlfriend; the only one I ever had, I regret to say."[81]

When Ted gathered the courage to show interest in a girl, he did so by playing bizarre practical jokes. Once he placed the skin of a cat that had been dissected in science class in a girl's locker. Another time he gave a classmate, JoAnn DeYoung, a rolled up piece of paper, twisted in the middle. She recalled, "When I [un]twisted it, there was like a pop. The thing had gone off, like he made a little hand bomb."[82]

Wanting their son to be happy, Ted's parents encouraged him to be involved in activities, so he played trombone in the high school band and joined the Coin Club, Biology Club, German Club, and Math Club. He felt superior to the other members, however, so soon stopped attending meetings. That left him with only two long-term interests: math and explosives. Former schoolmate Dale Eickelman remembered how he and Ted had successfully created a series of small bombs using scrounged ingredients and materials purchased at the local hardware store. "I remember Ted had the know-how of putting together things like batteries, wire leads, potassium nitrate and whatever and creating explosions."[83]

Changing Course

As he grew older Ted remained odd and aloof. At Harvard he lived in preppy Eliot House, but he avoided interacting with his housemates. "Ted had a special talent for avoiding relationships by moving quickly past groups of people and slamming the door behind him,"[84] former roommate Patrick McIntosh remembered.

Ted Kaczynski, third from right, pictured with his high school math club in 1958. Even as a young person, Kaczynski considered himself too good to associate with others his age.

When he moved to Berkeley he lived alone and made no friends. His students thought he was a poor teacher. They complained that his lectures were straight out of the textbook and that he refused to help them or listen to their concerns. "He absolutely refuses to answer questions,"[85] one wrote in an evaluation.

After leaving Berkeley Ted drifted from place to place looking for land. In 1971 he gave up the notion of living in Canada and, with David's financial help, bought acreage outside of Lincoln, Montana, a community of less than a thousand people. Surrounded by mountains and miles of dense forest, he built a tiny cabin with no electricity or plumbing and became known as the neighborhood hermit. By doing odd jobs, growing a vegetable garden, and killing wild animals for meat, he was able to live on less than three hundred dollars a year. In the summers he hiked and rode his bike to Lincoln, where he spent

In the 1970s Ted Kaczynski built this primitive cabin in the mountains of Lincoln, Montana. With no electricity or plumbing, this is where he lived until his capture in 1996.

hours in the library reading. In the winter when temperatures hovered around 0°F (-18°C), he huddled around his tiny wood stove or went underground into his root cellar to stay warm.

Anger Unleashed

Without anyone's knowledge, Ted also began striking out against people who disturbed the wilderness around him. He fired shots at small airplanes and helicopters that flew overhead. He strung wires across paths to bring down motorcycle and dirt bike riders. He poured sugar and sand into gasoline tanks of logging equipment.

As the years went on he became more of a recluse and distanced himself from his family. He ordered his mother Wanda to stop sending him care packages of books and food, although he accepted the money she and David sent periodically. When his family arrived on visits to Lincoln he disappeared without speaking to them. He insisted that he had been mistreated as a child and demanded apologies for imagined wrongs. He ignored David's letter informing him that their father had committed suicide in October 1990 after a prolonged battle with lung cancer.

David's marriage to Linda Patrik in July 1990 brought Ted's anger to the boiling point. Frustrated that he had never had a serious relationship with a woman, he resented his brother's happiness. It seemed like a betrayal. He insisted that his family cut all ties with him, stop visiting him, and stop writing him letters. He wrote to David in 1991, "I have got to know . . . that every last tie joining me to this stinking family has been cut FOREVER, and that I will never NEVER have to communicate with any of you again."[86]

Comparisons

Fearing that his brother was the Unabomber, yet knowing that he was deeply troubled, perhaps mentally ill, David hesitated to go to the police with his suspicions. Linda was insistent that something be done, however, so in October 1995 he hired private

A Desire for Revenge

Experts who studied the Unabomber case believed he was driven by his hatred of technology. In fact, that motive was secondary to a more personal one, as an entry from his journal, included in the book Unabomber: The Secret Life of Ted Kaczynski, *by Chris Waits and Dave Shors reveals:*

My motive for doing what I am going to do is simply personal revenge. I do not expect to accomplish anything by it. Of course, if my crime (and my reasons for committing it) gets any public attention, it may help to stimulate public interest in the technology question and thereby improve the chances of stopping technology before it is too late; on the other hand most people will probably be repelled by my crime. . . .

I have no way of knowing whether my action will do more good than harm. I certainly don't claim to be an altruist [unselfishly devoted to the welfare of others] or be acting for the "good" (whatever that is) of the human race. I act merely from a desire for revenge.

Quoted in Chris Waits and Dave Shors, *Unabomber: The Secret Life of Ted Kaczynski.* Helena, MT: Farcountry, 1999, pp. 264–65.

investigator Susan Swanson to research the Unabom case and compare it to details of Ted's life. To aid in her research, he provided her with dozens of letters that Ted had written to him and his parents in earlier years. In a short time Swanson realized that she could not rule Ted out as a suspect. She then turned to security consultant Clint Van Zandt, a former FBI behavioral science expert, and asked him to analyze the material and give his opinion.

With so much at stake, Van Zandt did not want to rely solely on his own judgment. He pulled together two independent teams that included a psychiatrist, a language expert, and two communications experts and gave them the manifesto and the letters to compare. Painstakingly, they analyzed the themes in the material. They also looked at elements such as spelling, word choice, grammar, and sentence structure. There were clear similarities to be seen. For instance, both Ted and the bomber mentioned the U.S. Commission on Violence, a group formed by President Lyndon Johnson in 1968 to address the growing problem of violence in America. Both referred to author L. Sprague DeCamp's history of great engineering feats entitled *Ancient Engineers*. Both used phrases such as "Big Government" and "Big Business, " and misspelled the same words—"wilfully" instead of "willfully," "analyse" instead of "analyze," and "instalment" instead of "installment."

Van Zandt and his teams did not feel they could write off the similarities as coincidence. Rather, they concluded that there was "at least a 60 percent chance that it was the same author"[87] who had written all the documents. After passing along that conclusion to Swanson, she suggested to David that he hire Bisceglie to get advice on how next to proceed. The attorney urged David to go with him to the FBI. David agreed but remembered, "It's agony when you love someone, when you want what's best for them, you want to protect them, and yet you are afraid that they may be hurting other people."[88]

Background Check

Skeptical of David's information, the FBI began their own background check on Ted. Almost immediately they discovered that his name was in their computer database as one of many Chicago students who had specialized in mathematics. He was also one who had shown interest in the radical environmental group Earth First! Because he had never publicly exhibited any dangerous or attention-grabbing behavior, however, his name had never come to the top of any list.

Now agents dug into his background in careful detail. They uncovered driver's license records that put him in Illinois at the time of the first bombings. They noted that bombings generally followed gifts of money received from his family, suggesting that he had used the funds to finance his terrorism. Other things seemed to fit, too—his intelligence, his antitechnology views, his interest in explosives, and his links to California. Investigators also discovered that he had lived in Utah for a time in the early 1980s, doing odd jobs and menial labor.

Undercover FBI agents traveled to Lincoln and talked with Ted's neighbors, who told of his hatred of loggers and devel-

Vandalism

Among his notebooks, Ted Kaczynski kept a secret "crime journal" written in code, which detailed the vandalism he carried out against his neighbors. The following decoded excerpt is included in Chris Waits's and Dave Shors's book Unabomber: The Secret Life of Ted Kaczynski:

Some (expletive) built a vacation house a few years ago . . . so one night in fall I sneaked over there, though they were home, and stole their chainsaw, buried it in a swamp. That was not enough, so couple weeks later when they had left the place, I chopped my way into their house, smashed up interior pretty thoroughly. It was a real luxury place. They also had a mobile home there. I broke into that too, found silver-painted motorcycle inside, smashed it up with their own ax. . . .

Week or so later, cops came up here and asked me if I had seen anyone fooling around with any buildings around here. . . . Probably they did not seriously suspect me, otherwise their questioning would not have been so perfunctory [casual]. . . . Who says crime doesn't pay? I feel very good about this. I am also pleased that I was so cool and collected in answering cops questions.

Quoted in Chris Waits and Dave Shors, *Unabomber: The Secret Life of Ted Kaczynski.* Helena, MT: Farcountry, 1999, pp. 204-205.

opers who had come into the area. They cited his regular visits to the town's single-room library. They also recalled that he sometimes disappeared for weeks at a time with no explanation. While none of that proved that Ted was the Unabomber, it did not rule him out, either.

Capture

With enough evidence to move ahead, the FBI decided it was time to take Ted into custody and search his cabin. On April 3, 1996, task force member Max Noel, FBI agent Tom McDaniel, and U.S. Forestry Service officer Jerry Burns pretended to be mining company surveyors with questions about a property line. They carefully approached the cabin, calling for Ted to come out.

When Ted opened the door to look at the map they carried, Burns grabbed his arm, and McDaniel put him in a headlock. He struggled and tried to pull free, but within seconds they had him in handcuffs. Agents then escorted him to a neighboring house where he was questioned. Finally, he was driven to the Lewis and Clark County jail in Helena, about fifty miles southeast of Lincoln. "We like the looks of this guy as the Unabomber, but we don't have make-or-break evidence yet," said one unnamed federal agent. "We have some writings that match up, but we don't have his tools yet. We want the irrefutable mother lode of evidence."[89]

> **By the Numbers**
>
> **10**
>
> The number of three-ring binders containing notes and diagrams of explosive devices, found in the Unabomber's cabin.

Investigators liked Ted's looks, but the public was shocked when his image appeared in newspapers and on television screens across the country. Douglas had predicted that when caught, the Unabomber would look like everyone's next-door neighbor. Ted was anything but that. Wild-haired and bearded, the former Berkeley professor looked haggard and exhausted when taken into custody. His clothes were tattered. He reeked of wood

Federal agents captured Ted Kaczynski on April 3, 1996. His filthy appearance was a long way from how most people would picture a former professor.

smoke, body odor, and unwashed clothes. FBI agent Candice DeLong recalled, "He . . . was so filthy that even his long eyelashes were caked with soot. . . . He was missing a front tooth."[90]

The Mother Lode

With Ted safely in custody, investigators began a search of his cabin. He had lived in the dark, smoky 10-foot by 12-foot room (3.05m by 3.66m) for twenty years, and it was packed to the ceiling with all the things he needed to survive and carry out his work. In addition to bedding, cooking utensils, and clothes, two walls were lined with books. Also in the room were neatly labeled containers of chemicals and smokeless powder, met-

A journal of coded messages that was found in the cabin was entered into evidence at Ted Kaczynski's trial.

al pipes of various sizes and shapes, copper tubing, and triggering devices—in short, all kinds of bomb-making materials. Ten three-ring binders were filled with bomb sketches and notes chronicling his explosive experiments. Along with rubber gloves, a small scale, and measuring spoons the investigators found the names and addresses of possible future targets—geneticists, psychiatrists, timber executives, and academics—and even a journal in which Ted admitted to the bombings.

The investigators found a completed bomb under the bed, neatly packaged and ready to be mailed. In other parts of the shack they found a copy of the manifesto and three manual typewriters, one of which was later matched to letters sent to Hoge and other editors. Law professor and news commentator Laurie Levenson observed, "I have never seen one little shack with so much evidence. It's the ultimate FBI scavenger hunt. This is his life, his entire existence—it's his life's work."[91]

When investigators raided Ted Kaczynski's cabin they discovered a bomb, packaged and ready to be mailed to the next victim.

To law enforcement agents, their eighteen-year search seemed to be drawing to a close. Still, they remembered that in the United States, a suspect is always assumed to be innocent until proven guilty in a court of law. Theodore Kaczynski might look like the Unabomber, but they could take nothing for granted. So they contained their excitement and focused on correctly documenting and processing all the evidence they found. As one unnamed law enforcement official said, "Stay tuned. There's enough about him to make it a real possibility, but we've had dry holes before. I'm not getting my hopes too high, but I'm hopeful."[92]

CHAPTER 6

Case Closed

The hunt for the Unabomber had ended, but the work of bringing him to trial had just begun. Legal wrangling over the case lasted two years. For a time experts thought that it might take a decade to satisfy multiple state demands for justice. Defense attorney Ron Kuby commented in 1996: "The Federal Government has enough separate charges in separate jurisdictions that they could lose every single case and still keep the guy on trial for the rest of his life."[93]

"Not a Perfect World"

Legal proceedings began almost immediately after Ted's arrest. As he sat in jail in Helena, attorneys Tony Gallagher and Michael Donahoe—members of the nonprofit group Federal Defenders of Montana—stepped forward and offered to represent him in court. Information about the contents of the cabin had been leaked to the press, so they filed a motion to dismiss all charges based on the impossibility of finding an impartial jury when the case went to trial. Donahoe wrote in his motion: "The possibility that he [Theodore Kaczynski] could ever be afforded anything that might remotely resemble (the fair trial) process has been forever lost."[94]

U.S. attorney Bernard Hubley agreed that leaks were inappropriate, but argued that they were not serious enough to exempt Ted from prosecution. He pointed out, "The government has been unable to find a single federal case in which a court has suppressed evidence or completely barred a criminal prosecution based on pre-indictment publicity.[95]

U.S. District judge Charles C. Lovell in Montana agreed. He denied Donahoe's motion, stating, "The defendant is not

FBI agents guard the entrance to Ted Kaczynski's property near Lincoln, Montana, shortly after his capture in April 1996.

entitled to perfect treatment. It's not a perfect world. He is entitled to fair treatment. I think he has received fair treatment."[96]

A Huge Task

Before Donahoe and Gallagher could plan a new defense, the Justice Department took responsibility out of their hands. In June 1996 it assigned federal attorney Quin Denvir to head Ted's defense team. Denvir was highly qualified to take on the challenging task. He was the head of the Sacramento defender's office, in charge of some twenty attorneys there. He had argued before the California Supreme Court more than twenty-five times and had succeeded in getting the court to reverse three guilty verdicts in death penalty cases. Former California Surpreme Court justice Cruz Reynoso testified, "I consider him one of the best lawyers, most ethical lawyers I ever worked with. [He is] a real craftsman, a person of great sense of justice."[97]

Denvir invited Donahoe and Gallagher to participate in future proceedings, but the former declined, and the latter chose to remain in Montana and do what he could on the case from there. Thus, Denvir relied on his assistants and, in mid-July 1996, added renowned defense attorney Judy Clarke to his team.

All were aware that a huge task lay before them. They had to analyze a mountain of evidence found in the cabin. They had to go through 11 million pages of documents and photos in almost sixty thousand files that had accumulated over eighteen years. To give them adequate time, Judge Garland E. Burrell Jr., who had been assigned to oversee the trial, gave them a year to prepare and set November 12, 1997, as the opening date.

"The Best Evidence, the Best Case"

About the same time Denvir was assigned to the case, a California federal grand jury returned the first indictments against Ted. On June 18 he was charged with transporting and mailing bombs as well as the murder of Scrutton in Sacramento. He was also charged with the attacks on Epstein and Gelernter and with killing timber lobbyist Murray. In addition to the

Defense attorneys Judy Clarke, left, and Quin Denvir had the tremendous challenge of representing accused Unabomber, Ted Kaczynski, during his trial.

How a Federal Criminal Case Is Processed

Those who break federal laws go through the following process as their case moves through the criminal justice system:

1 **Arrest:** Suspect is taken into legal custody after commission of a crime.

2 **Initial appearance in court:** Suspect is advised of charges filed and is provided with a lawyer if necessary.

3 **Grand jury review:** Evidence presented by prosecutor is reviewed to determine if there is cause for trial.

4 **Indictment:** Grand jury files concise, factual written statements of the time, place, and manner of the crimes.

5 **Arraignment:** Defendant hears the formal indictment in court and is asked to enter a plea of guilty, not guilty, or no contest.

6 **Pretrial motions and conferences:** Attorneys present requests for evidence, to suppress evidence, to change trial venue, etc.

7 **Trial by jury:** Defense and prosecution attorneys present evidence.

8 **Sentencing:** If the defendant is found guilty, court imposes sentence.

9 **Appeal:** The convicted can apply for review of the case by a higher court.

California charges, on June 28, 1996, the federal government added three more counts for incidents in Tennessee, Utah, and Michigan. On October 1 New Jersey indicted him for the murder of Mosser.

Federal attorney Robert J. Cleary of New Jersey was assigned to prosecute the government's case. Cleary pulled together a team of attorneys from across the country that included R. Steven Lapham from Sacramento and Stephen Freccero from San Francisco. Both had worked with the Unabom task force since 1993 and knew the case. Lapham observed, "This is a big case nationally, but no different from any case we have to try. Our job is to put the evidence together and present it to a jury."[98]

California would be the site of the first trial. Two men had been murdered in California. Many of the bombs had been mailed from California. Several victims who would testify at the trial lived in the state. In addition, the Justice Department had authorized prosecutors to seek the death penalty, and California law permitted execution by gas or lethal injection. "[In California, we have] the best evidence, the best case, the rules of the court,"[99] said Justice Department spokesman John Russell.

Mental Illness Defense

As preparations went forward, more facts regarding Ted's involvement came to light. Receipts and eyewitness reports tied him to suspicious locales on or about the dates that bombs were mailed. Entries in his journal such as "I intend to start killing people," and "Here I am going to confess to—or, to be more accurate, brag about—some misdeeds I have committed in the past few years"[100] not only emphasized that he had premeditated his crimes, but that he had no remorse for what he did.

Faced with those facts, Denvir and Clarke decided that even the most impartial jury would find Ted guilty of being the Unabomber. They believed he could perhaps avoid the death penalty, however, if it could be demonstrated that he was mentally ill. To gain facts to support a mental illness defense, Denvir asked psychiatrist

By the Numbers

600

The number of California residents summoned to be potential jurists in the Unabomber trial.

83

Ted Kaczynski's journals and other evidence were studied by a psychiatrist to determine if he was mentally ill. Pictured is one of Kaczynski's journals that outlines where he had hidden food around his cabin.

David Vernon Foster to interview Ted and the Kaczynskis and to study Ted's journals, letters, medical records, and family history.

David and Wanda strongly supported that strategy. David emphasized that his brother had long suffered from "unpredictable mood swings, a preoccupation with disease, extreme phobias, compulsive thinking and an inability to let go of minutiae [details]. One senses a psyche that feels itself terribly isolated and threatened in the world."[101] David and his mother also believed that it would be outrageous for Ted to be put to death if his actions were a result of illness. David said, "I can't condone what he did . . . [but] it would be very, very difficult to live with

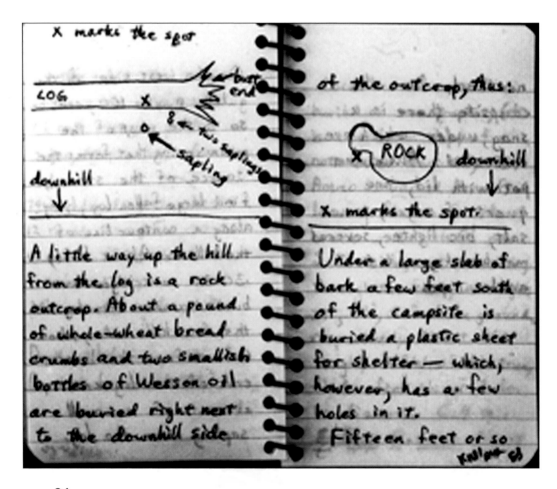

myself knowing that I had delivered my injured, disturbed brother over to be killed." [102]

Plagued by Delusions

In November 1997 Foster began his evaluation of Ted and his writings. Interviews with the defendant lasted only three hours, however. They were cut short when Ted became extremely angry and upset at the mere mention of mental illness.

Foster had no difficulty diagnosing Ted as having paranoid schizophrenia—a severe brain disorder that causes delusions, feelings of persecution, disturbances in thinking and communication, and social isolation. He stated,

> The delusions that plague Mr. Kaczynski have invaded all spheres of his life and dictate his actions. He believes . . . that technological society intends to destroy him and others like him. According to his writings, Mr. Kaczynski chronically views accidental or intentional personal contact with other people, newspaper articles, scientific advances, commercial and residential development, air traffic, and radio and television broadcasts as threats to his survival. [103]

Foster also pointed out that Ted's disorder manifested itself in his fear of being considered mentally ill and his strong opposition to being evaluated by psychiatrists. The mere thought of it made him highly agitated. Foster wrote, "In Mr. Kaczynski's perception, psychiatrists seek to eliminate free will and personal autonomy by creating a population that is wholly compliant with the needs of an omnipotent [all-powerful] system." [104]

"We Are All Very Unhappy"

Ted's attitude became Denvir and Clarke's biggest hurdle in the coming months. As the trial date of November 1997 approached

---

By the Numbers

7 x 12 FEET (2.1 x 3.7 m)

The size of Theodore Kaczynski's prison cell in Florence, Colorado.

Becoming an Attorney

Job Description:

Attorneys are both advisers and advocates for their clients and can act as defense or prosecution lawyers in criminal and civil trials. They advise their clients regarding a multitude of issues in both business and personal matters. They conduct most of their work in offices, libraries, and courtrooms, but also travel to gather evidence and meet with clients. Hours and workloads vary from standard schedules to significant amounts of overtime.

Personal Qualifications:

Aspiring attorneys must enjoy taking responsibility and working with people. Perseverance, creativity, and advanced reasoning skills are required.

Education:

Aspiring attorneys must earn a bachelor's degree from an accredited college or university. They must then complete at least three years of law school in order to earn their doctor of law degree. After graduation they must pass a state bar examination, which includes questions on law and ethics. They must also remain current on legal and nonlegal developments that may affect their area of practice.

Salary:

Attorneys can earn between $40,000 and $150,000 annually.

and jury selection began, Cleary insisted that a government psychiatrist needed to examine Ted. Without that exam, the prosecution team did not have all the evidence it needed. It could not know if Denvir and Clarke were misrepresenting Ted's mental state or not.

Burrell agreed and ordered an exam be carried out. Ted, however, refused to cooperate. He denied that he had a problem and grew angry when the issue was discussed. His attorneys tried to convince him of the wisdom of the course. If the prosecution could not call its own expert witness to testify regarding Ted's mental state, the judge would likely refuse to allow the defense to do so, too. That would weaken their case and put Ted in jeopardy of conviction and the death penalty.

Ted could not be swayed. Instead, he wrote letters to Burrell, complaining that his lawyers were not representing him as he wished. Denvir observed, "This is obviously a major problem. We are all very unhappy and sad to be in this position, but we are in the position. We have to do, I guess, what we can."[105]

Power Struggle

Despite the complications, on January 5, 1998, a jury was seated and everyone gathered for opening day of trial. Ted's determination to avoid a mental illness defense stopped proceedings before opening arguments could take place, however. He rose and asked Burrell to allow him to fire his attorneys and replace them with new ones. Burrell denied the request, in part because selecting a new team and waiting for them to prepare their defense meant another year of delay. Frustrated and deeply troubled by what he feared was going to be said about him in the coming days, Ted then attempted to hang himself in his cell on the evening of January 7.

Despite the gravity of the incident, he suffered no serious injury and was well enough to be in court the next morning. There, he demanded that the judge allow him to represent himself at trial. "It is a very heartfelt reaction to the mental health defense," Clarke said. "He feels he has no choice because his present counsel intends to present him in a light of mental illness. [That is a defense] that he simply cannot endure." [106]

Unsure if Kaczynski was competent to represent himself, Burrell issued an ultimatum. Either he allowed himself to be evaluated by a government-chosen psychiatrist or he would be immediately taken to a psychiatric ward and evaluated there. Faced with those alternatives, Ted agreed to cooperate.

The Compromise

On January 12, 1998, Federal Bureau of Prisons psychiatrist Sally Johnson arrived in Sacramento to begin her evaluation of the prisoner. She met with Ted and his lawyers, administered several tests, interviewed his family, and studied his journals, letters, and other documents. On January 17, 1998, she issued her findings to the court. The prisoner had superior intelligence, but he suffered from severe schizophrenia, which had negatively impacted his life and career. He had never had hallucinations, but his delusions about the harmful effects of technology were all-controlling. His paranoia made him extremely sensitive.

Even the absence of encouragement was seen as deliberate humiliation or persecution.

Johnson believed that Ted understood the charges against him and realized the penalties he faced if found guilty. She concluded that he was competent to stand trial despite the fact that he was mentally ill. Nevertheless, she cautioned the court to remember that Ted would likely be a challenging defendant. She wrote, "He will continue to focus on detail and be reluctant to separate out useful detail from unnecessary detail. He will continue to demonstrate his ambivalence and suspiciousness."[107]

Such was the case when trial resumed on January 22. Again, Ted brought proceedings to a halt with a demand to represent himself. Faced with a situation that threatened to push everyone's patience to the breaking point, Denvir and Clarke took their client aside and convinced him to agree to a plea bargain. He would plead guilty to all the charges in exchange for a life sentence with no possibility of parole or appeal. Cleary, after consulting with bombing victims and their families, agreed. They all concluded that "justice could best be served by an immediate guarantee that the defendant would spend the rest of his life behind bars." [108]

Last Words

On May 4, 1998, Ted was sentenced to four life terms in prison and instructed to pay $15 million in restitution to his victims. Because he was poor it seemed unlikely that the money would ever be paid. When David learned that he would receive the

---

"Make This Sentence Bullet Proof"

Although some of his victims forgave Ted Kaczynski at his sentencing hearing, Susan Mosser, whose husband died in December 1994, did not. Her words to the judge are included in journalist Ted Ottley's article "Back to Court":

Nails. Razor blades. Wire. Pipe. Batteries. Everyday household items. Pack them together, explode them with the force of a bullet from a rifle, and you have a bomb. Hold it in your hand while it is exploding, as my husband Tom did, and you have unbearable pain . . . the excruciating pain of a hundred nails, cut up razor blades and metal fragments perforating your heart, shearing off your fingers, burning your skin, fracturing your skull, and driving shrapnel into your brain. . . .

Please, your honor, make this sentence bullet proof, bomb proof. . . . Lock him so far down that when he does die, he'll be closer to hell. That's where the devil belongs!

Quoted in Ted Ottley, "Back to Court," Crime Library, 2007. www.crimelibrary.com/terrorists_spies/terrorists/kaczynski/14.html.

$1 million reward offered by the Justice Department, however, he donated half to the victims. The other half was set aside to pay Ted's huge legal bills. "There is no way any amount of money could compensate them [the victims] for their pain," David stated, "but I hope this will help provide some sense of resolution to the people who were harmed by my brother."[109]

Before sentencing, Burrell also gave victims the opportunity to speak to Ted. "Ted, I do not hate you. I forgave you a long time ago,"[110] said Wright. Epstein was more condemnatory. "You saved your own neck, but you did everything, and more, and you did it in cold blood."[111] And Lois Epstein stated, "You are the person who sent a bomb to my home in an attempt to murder a man who has never done you a moment's harm. . . . That you have been sentenced to life imprisonment without the possibility of appeal or parole is, in my opinion, almost too kind."[112]

This courtroom sketch depicts defense attorney Judy Clarke, left, and an unemotional Ted Kaczynski as he was sentenced to four life terms in prison on May 4, 1998.

Their words had no apparent effect on Ted. He listened unemotionally, then stated: "At a later time I expect to respond at length to the sentencing memorandum and also the many falsehoods that have been propagated about me. I only ask that people reserve their judgment about me and about the Unabom case until all the facts have been made public."[113] While he was speaking, Murray's family got up and left the courtroom. "I walked out because there is nothing that he could say that I was willing to hear," said Murray's widow, Connie. "He has no concept or understanding of what he has done."[114]

By the Numbers

400

The number of people who have corresponded with Theodore Kaczynski since his arrest in 1996.

Supermax

After sentencing, Ted was transported to the maximum-security federal prison—also known as "Supermax"—in Florence, Colorado. As Prisoner Number 04475-046, he lives in what he considers relative luxury after his years in Montana. His tiny cell is warm and well lighted. It has a toilet, a concrete desk and stool, and a thirteen-inch television that shows recreational, educational, and religious programs. He showers every other day and gets freshly laundered bedding and clothing three times a week. He spends his time writing letters and reading, choosing from books and magazines delivered to him from the prison library.

Bedtime is 10 P.M. and wake-up call is at 6 A.M. when breakfast is delivered. "The food here, believe it or not, is pretty good,"[115] he says. Several days a week he is allowed ninety minutes of recreation, and this is the only time he has contact with other prisoners. Most are "celebrities" such as himself and include FBI spy Robert Hanssen, Mafia boss Salvatore "Sammy the Bull" Gravano, and Ramzi Yousef, the mastermind of the 1993 World Trade Center bombing. Ted observes, "These people are not what you would think of as criminal types. I mean, they don't seem to be very angry people. They're considerate of others. Some of them are quite intelligent."[116]

Convicted Unabomber Ted Kaczynski, pictured in 1999 at the Supermax federal prison in Florence, Colorado, will spend the rest of his life in prison.

Despite the small comforts, Kaczynski never forgets that he has lost the freedom he valued so much. He is monitored by motion detectors, cameras, and guards twenty-four hours a day. He is strip-searched and shackled when he leaves his cell. And he has no contact with his beloved nature, not even a glimpse of the Rocky Mountains from his prison window. He observes, "I'm not depressed or downcast, and I have things I can do that I consider productive. . . . And yet the knowledge that I'm locked up here and likely to remain so for the rest of my life—it ruins it. And I don't want to live long. I would rather get the death penalty than spend the rest of my life in prison."[117]

Tragic Figure

Ted remains deeply angry with his family, with whom he refuses to communicate. He is convinced that beneath his brother's caring exterior is "a marked strain of resentment [and] jealousy over the fact that our parents valued me more highly." He also believes that David turned him in to the FBI as a way to get even. "It's quite true that he is troubled by guilt over what he's done. But I think his sense of guilt is outweighed by his satisfaction at having finally gotten revenge on big brother."[118]

When asked if he feels guilt, however, David denies it. "Guilt suggests a very clear conviction of wrongdoing, and certainly I don't feel that I did wrong," he says.[119] Members of the task force, who hunted the Unabomber for so many years, agree with David. They understand his difficult battle with his conscience and how he will always regret that he was not able to protect his brother. But they admire his decision, because they are convinced that Ted would have taken more innocent lives if he had remained free. DeLong summed up the general feeling when she wrote, "To my mind, David Kaczynski deserved to be named Man of the Year."[120]

If David is a heroic figure, Ted is a tragic one—a man with a great deal of potential who somehow went wrong. Rather than using his brilliance to help solve the world's problems, he was driven by his illness to fight a one-man battle against progress. As Suino, injured in 1985, stated at Ted's sentencing, "He has actually become the very thing he once seemed to fear. Not a victim of progress, but an empty machine, devoid of conscience."[121]

Notes

Introduction: Eighteen-Year Manhunt

1. Quoted in Unabomber Trial.com, "John E. Hauser, Bombing Victim," 2007. www.unabombertrial.com/players/hauser.html.

2. Quoted in *Nova*, "Bombing in America," March 25, 1997. www.pbs.org/wgbh/nova/transcripts/2310tbomb.html.

3. Quoted in Richard Paddock, "Unabomber Threatens LAX Flights, Then Calls It a Prank," *Los Angeles Times*, June 29, 1995, p. A1.

4. Quoted in Meghan Piercy, "Manhunt for a Terrorist," University of Montana School of Journalism, Spring 2006. www.umt.edu/Journalism/student_work/unabomber/fbi.htm.

5. Quoted in John Yemma, "Brilliant Misfit Caught in Changing Times; Unabom Suspect Stayed Aloof on Turbulent '60s Campuses, Then Rejected Society," *Boston Globe*, April 7, 1996, p.1.

6. Quoted in Unabomber Trial.com, "David Kaczynski, Bomber's Brother," 2007. www.unabombertrial.com/players/david.html.

Chapter 1: Targets Coast-to-Coast

7. Quoted in Clifford J. Levy, "Bombing in New Jersey," *New York Times*, December 13, 1994, p. A1.

8. Quoted in *Nova*, "Bombing in America." www.pbs.org/wgbh/nova/transcripts/2310tbomb.html.

9. Quoted in Ted Ottley, "Come Fly with Me," *Crime Library*, 2007. www.crimelibrary.com/terrorists_spies/terrorists/kaczynski/3.html.

10. Quoted in Unabomber Trial.com, "Package Bomb Injures United Airline Chief," June 11, 1980. www.unabombertrial.com/archive/pre1995/061180.html.

11. Quoted in Robert Graysmith, *Unabomber: A Desire to Kill*. Washington, DC: Regnery, 1997, p. 161.

12. Quoted in Graysmith, *Unabomber: A Desire to Kill*, p. 86.

13. Quoted in Graysmith, *Unabomber: A Desire to Kill*, p. 186.

14. Quoted in Graysmith, *Unabomber: A Desire to Kill*, pp. 201–202.

15. Quoted in Ted Ottley, "A Trio for Ted," *Crime Library*, 2007. www.crimelibrary.com/terrorists_spies/terrorists/kaczynski/7.html.

16. Quoted in Robert D. Davila, "Quirk in Routine Brought Bomb, Lobbyist Together," *Sacramento Bee*, April 25, 1995, p. A11.

17. Quoted in Bill Lindelof and Sam Stanton, "Unabomber Kills Again, Timber Lobbyist

Slain in Capital," *Sacramento Bee*, April 25, 1995, p. A1.

18. Quoted in Lindelof and Stanton, "Unabomber Kills Again," p. A1.

19. Quoted in *Nova*, "Bombing in America."

Chapter 2: Scraps and Splinters

20. Quoted in Steve Macko, "The Chicago Police Department Bomb Squad," Emergency Net News Service, January 27, 1996. www.emergency.com/CHBMBSQD.htm.

21. Raymond E. Foster, "Crime Scene Investigation," Police One.com, March 17, 2005. www.policeone.com/police-products/crime-scene-investigation/articles/99554.

22. Quoted in Gina Barton, "Exploding Myths: Bomb Experts Rely on Smarts, Not Wire Cutters," *Milwaukee Journal Sentinel*, July 24, 2004. www.jsonline.com/story/index.aspx?id=245284.

23. Quoted in Ken Foskett, "Lab Is Nerve Center for Solving Bombings," *Atlanta Journal and Constitution*, March 30, 1997. www.unabombers.com/VanPac/v97-03-30-SqareEndPlates-1.htm.

24. Quoted in *Nova*, "Bombing in America."

25. Quoted in Ralph Blumenthal and N.R. Kleinfield, "Death in the Mail: Tracking a Killer," *New York Times*, December 18, 1994, p. 49.

26. Quoted in *Fortune*, "Closing in on the Unabomber," August 21, 1995, p. 92.

27. Quoted in Catherine Bowman and Michael Taylor, "Fatal Bomb Linked to 15 Others; Deadly Package Linked to New Jersey Ad Man," *San Francisco Chronicle*, December 12, 1994, p. A1.

28. Quoted in Nancy Gibbs, Richard Lacayo, Lance Morrow, Jill Smolowe, and David Van Biema, *Mad Genius: The Odyssey, Pursuit, and Capture of the Unabomber Suspect*. New York: Warner, 1996, p. 71.

29. Quoted in *St. Petersburg Times*, "Police: Postal Bomber's Work Increasingly Devious, Deadly," December 14, 1994, p. 3A.

30. Quoted in Nancy Gibbs, "Tracking Down the Unabomber," *Time*, April 15, 1996, p. 38.

31. Quoted in *Nova*, "Bombing in America."

32. John Douglas and Mark Olshaker, *Unabomber: On the Trail of America's Most-Wanted Serial Killer*. New York: Pocket Books, 1996, p. 155.

Chapter 3: A Shadowy Profile

33. Quoted in Lea Winerman, "Criminal Profiling: The Reality Behind the Myth," *Monitor on Psychology*, July/August 2004, p. 66.

34. Quoted in Winerman, "Criminal Profiling," p. 66.

35. Douglas and Olshaker, *Unabomber: On the Trail*, pp. 38–39.

36. Douglas and Olshaker, *Unabomber: On the Trail*, p. 38.

37. Douglas and Olshaker, *Unabomber: On the Trail*, p. 36.

38. Douglas and Olshaker, *Unabomber: On the Trail*, p. 64.

39. Quoted in Graysmith, *Unabomber: A Desire to Kill*, p. 291.

40. Quoted in Gibbs, "Tracking Down the Unabomber," p. 38.

41. Quoted in Gibbs et al., *Mad Genius*, p. 96.

42. Quoted in Ottley, "Come Fly with Me."

43. Quoted in *USA Today*, "List of 200 Top Suspects Doesn't Include 70's Radicals," November 13, 1996. www.usatoday.com/news/index/una9.htm.

44. Quoted in Blumenthal and Kleinfield, "Death in the Mail," p. 49.

45. Quoted in Terry D. Turchie Affidavit, "Bomb #7 Victim: Diogenes J. Angelakos, University of California, Berkeley (7/7/82)," April 3, 1996. www.unabombertrial.com/documents/bomb_7.html.

46. Quoted in Robert Rudolph, "'The Biggest Mistake of His Life'; Letters, Manifesto Haunt Bomb Suspect," *Star-Ledger* (Newark, NJ), April 6, 1996, p. 1.

Chapter 4: The Bomber's Words

47. Quoted in Michael D. Lemonick, "The Bomb Is in the Mail," *Time*, May 8, 1995, p. 70.

48. Quoted in Graysmith, *Unabomber: A Desire to Kill*, p. 101.

49. Quoted in Unabomber Trial.com, "Letter Sent to the *New York Times*," April 24, 1995. www.unabombertrial.com/manifesto/nytletter.html.

50. Quoted in Patrick Hoge and Jane Meredith Adams, "Bomber Seen as Arrogant Crusader," *Sacramento Bee*, April 28, 1995, p. B1.

51. Quoted in Unabomber Trial.com, "Turchie Affidavit," April 3, 1996. www.unabombertrial.com/documents/turchie_affidavit.html.

52. Quoted in Unabomber Trial.com, "The Investigation," 2007. www.unabombertrial.com/investigation/investigation.html.

53. Lloyd R. Smith, "Terrorism Hits the Heartland," *Disaster Recovery Journal*, April 19, 1995. www.drj.com/special/ok.html.

54. Quoted in Graysmith, *Unabomber: A Desire to Kill*, p. 297.

55. Quoted in Graysmith, *Unabomber: A Desire to Kill*, p. 303.

56. Quoted in Douglas and Olshaker, *Unabomber: On the Trail*, p. 181.

57. Quoted in Unabomber Trial.com, "Letter Sent to the *New York Times*."

58. Quoted in Unabomber Trial.com, "Letter Sent to the *New York Times*."

59. Quoted in Unabomber Trial.com, "Letter Sent to the *New York Times*."

60. Quoted in Unabomber Trial.com, "Letter Sent to the *New York Times*."

61. Quoted in Unabomber Trial.com, "Letter Sent to the *New York Times*."

62. Quoted in Douglas and Olshaker, *Unabomber: On the Trail*, p. 244.

63. Quoted in Douglas and Olshaker, *Unabomber: On the Trail*, p. 229.

64. Quoted in Douglas and Olshaker, *Unabomber: On the Trail*, p. 246.

65. Quoted in Douglas and Olshaker, *Unabomber: On the Trail*, p. 198.

66. Quoted in Douglas and Olshaker, *Unabomber: On the Trail*, p. 252.

67. Quoted in Graysmith, *Unabomber: A Desire to Kill*, p. 351.

68. Quoted in *Mobile Register*, "Bomber's Demand Puts Newspapers in Quandary; Writer Says He Will Kill Again if Papers Don't Publish His Manifesto," July 1, 1995, p. A11.

69. Quoted in Graysmith, *Unabomber: A Desire to Kill*, p. 354.

70. Gibbs et al., *Mad Genius*, p. 118.

71. Quoted in Gibbs et al., *Mad Genius*, pp. 117–18.

72. David Kaczynski, "The Death Penalty Up Close and Personal," New Yorkers Against the Death Penalty, 2007. www.nyadp. org/main/david.html.

Chapter 5: The Montana Hermit

73. Quoted in David Stout, "US Seeking Death for Unabom Suspect," *New York Times*, May 16, 1997, p. A1.

74. Quoted in Graysmith, *Unabomber: A Desire to Kill*, p. 363.

75. Quoted in Gibbs et al., *Mad Genius*, p. 246.

76. Quoted in Michael Taylor, "'Your Brother Ted Might Be the Unabomber,' David Kaczynski Recounts His Anguish in Solving the Case," *San Francisco Chronicle*, April 14, 2004, p. B3.

77. Quoted in Robert D. McFadden, "From a Child of Promise to the Unabom Suspect," *New York Times*, May 26, 1996, p. 1.1.

78. Quoted in Unabomber Trial.com, "Theodore Kaczynski: The Suspect," 2007. www.unabombertrial.com/players/ kaczynski.html.

79. Quoted in Unabomber Trial.com, "Theodore Kaczynski: The Suspect."

80. Quoted in Unabomber Trial.com, "Theodore Kaczynski: The Suspect."

81. Quoted in Stephen J. Dubner, "I Don't Want to Live Long. I Would Rather Get the Death Penalty than Spend the Rest of My Life in Prison," *Time*, October 18, 1999, p. 44.

82. Quoted in Unabomber Trial.com, "Classmates Recall Suspect's Bomblets, Wood Connection, Immaturity," April 8, 1996. www.unabombertrial.com/archive/1996/0 40896-3.html.

83. Quoted in Gibbs, "Tracking Down the Unabomber," p. 38.

84. Quoted in Gibbs, "Tracking Down the Unabomber," p. 38.

85. Quoted in McFadden, "From a Child of Promise to the Unabom Suspect," p. 1.

86. Quoted in Graysmith, *Unabomber: A Desire to Kill*, pp. 115–16.

87. Quoted in Serge F. Kovaleski and Pierre Thomas, "Brother of Unabomber Suspect Had Hired Private Investigator," *Washington Post*, April 9, 1996, p. 2.

88. Quoted in Unabomber Trial.com, "David Kaczynski, Bomber's Brother."

89. Quoted in Wes Smith and Gary Marx, "U.S. Seizes Unabomber Suspect; Family's Tip Leads FBI to Recluse," *Chicago Tribune*, April 4, 1996, p. 1.

90. Quoted in Ted Ottley, "Montana Hermit," *Crime Library*, 2007. www.crimelibrary. com/terrorists_spies/terrorists/kaczynski/ 10.html.

91. Quoted in Graysmith, *Unabomber: A Desire to Kill*, p. 427.

92. Quoted in David Jackson, "FBI Detains Man in Unabomber Case; Charges Hinge on Montana Search," *Dallas Morning News*, April 4, 1996, p. A1.

Chapter 6: Case Closed

93. Quoted in Gibbs et al., *Mad Genius*, p. 147.

94. Quoted in Gibbs et al., *Mad Genius*, p. 146.

95. Quoted in CNN.com, "Judge Refuses to Dismiss Charge Against Unabom Suspect," April 19, 1996. www.cnn.com/ US/9604/19/unabom.hearing/index.html.

96. Quoted in Gibbs et al., *Mad Genius*, p. 146.

97. Quoted in Unabomber Trial.com, "Quin Denvir, Federal Public Defender," 2007. www.unabombertrial.com/players/ denvir.html.

98. Quoted in Unabomber Trial.com, "R. Steven Lapham, First Assistant US Attorney," 2007. www.unabombertrial.com/players/lapham.html.

99. Quoted in *USA Today*, "Feds Focusing on Sacramento for Potential Trial Site," November 13, 1996. www.usatoday.com/news/index/una46.htm.

100. Quoted in *New York Times*, "Kaczynski Worried About 'Sick' Label," November 20, 1997, p. A18.

101. Quoted in Graysmith, *Unabomber: A Desire to Kill*, p. 450.

102. Quoted in Graysmith, *Unabomber: A Desire to Kill*, p. 455.

103. Quoted in Unabomber Trial.com, "Declaration of David Vernon Foster, MD," November 12, 1997. www.unabombertrial.com/documents/psyche_exhibitA.html.

104. Quoted in Unabomber Trial.com, "Declaration of David Vernon Foster, MD."

105. Quoted in Denny Walsh, "Kaczynski Cites Defense Concerns; Unhappy with Team's Actions," *Sacramento Bee*, December 27, 1997, p. A1.

106. Quoted in Cynthia Hubert and Denny Walsh, "Kaczynski Reportedly Tries to Take Own Life," *Sacramento Bee*, January 9, 1998, p. A1.

107. Quoted in Unabomber Trial.com, "Psychiatric Competency Report of Dr. Sally C. Johnson," September 11, 1998. www.unabombertrial.com/documents/psych_report3.html.

108. Quoted in Cynthia Hubert and Denny Walsh, "Kaczynski Pleads Guilty to Blasts; Unabomber Will Spend Rest of His Life Behind Bars," *Sacramento Bee*, January 23, 1998, p. A1.

109. Quoted in Cynthia Hubert and Claire Cooper, "Unabom Reward Paid to Brother; David Kaczynski Plans Trust Fund for Victims," *Sacramento Bee*, August 21, 1998, p. B1.

110. Quoted in Cynthia Hubert, "Unabomber Gets Life Sentence; Victims Tell Kaczynski of Their Anguish," *Sacramento Bee*, May 5, 1998, p. A1.

111. Quoted in Hubert, "Unabomber Gets Life Sentence," p. A1.

112. Quoted in Hubert, "Unabomber Gets Life Sentence," p. A1.

113. Quoted in Hubert, "Unabomber Gets Life Sentence," p. A1.

114. Quoted in Hubert, "Unabomber Gets Life Sentence," p. A1.

115. Quoted in Dubner, "I Don't Want to Live Long," p. 44.

116. Quoted in Dubner, "I Don't Want to Live Long," p. 44.

117. Quoted in Dubner, "I Don't Want to Live Long," p. 44.

118. Quoted in Dubner, "I Don't Want to Live Long," p. 44.

119. Quoted in Dubner, "I Don't Want to Live Long," p. 44.

120. Quoted in Ted Ottley, "Brother and Hero," *Crime Library*, 2007. www.crimelibrary.com/terrorists_spies/terrorists/kaczynski/15.html.

121. Quoted in Ted Ottley, "Back to Court," *Crime Library*, 2007. www.crimelibrary.com/terrorists_spies/terrorists/kaczynski/14.html.

For More Information

Books

John Douglas and Mark Olshaker, *Unabomber: On the Trail of America's Most-Wanted Serial Killer*. New York: Pocket Books, 1996. Rushed to print immediately after the capture of Kaczynski, the book contains a great deal of material about other serial killers Douglas has profiled. Includes information about the Unabom attacks, Kaczynski's letters, and the complete manifesto.

Nancy Gibbs, Richard Lacayo, Lance Morrow, Jill Smolowe, and David Van Biema, *Mad Genius: The Odyssey, Pursuit, and Capture of the Unabomber Suspect*. New York: Warner, 1996. A good overview of the Unabomber story, put together by a staff of twelve reporters and editors from *Time* magazine in just eleven days.

Chris Waits and Dave Shors, *Unabomber: The Secret Life of Ted Kaczynski*. Helena, MT: Farcountry, 1999. The story of Ted Kaczynski's years in Montana, written by one of his neighbors. Includes excerpts from his journals.

Periodicals

Stephen J. Dubner, "I Don't Want to Live Long. I Would Rather Get the Death Penalty than Spend the Rest of My Life in Prison," *Time*, October 18, 1999.

Nancy Gibbs, "Tracking Down the Unabomber," *Time*, April 15, 1996.

Web Sites

CNN: The Unabomb Case (www.cnn.com/SPECIALS/1997/unabomb). Background on Kaczynski, trial transcripts, an interactive map, and more.

Court TV's Crime Library (www.crimelibrary.com/index.html). In-depth coverage of serial killers and other notorious criminals including Theodore Kaczynski.

Sacramento Bee: **Unabomber** (www.unabombertrial.com). News articles, multimedia, court transcripts, a timeline of events, and profiles of those involved.

Index

Picture Credits

About the Author

Diane Yancey lives in the Pacific Northwest with her husband, Michael; their dog, Gelato; and their cats, Lily and Newton. She has written more than twenty-five books for middle-grade and high-school readers, including *Murder, Forensic Anthropology, The Case of the Green River Killer,* and *Tracking Serial Killers.*